Algebra Made Simple
High School

Table of Contents

Frank Schaffer
An imprint of Carson-Dellosa Publishing LLC
PO Box 35665
Greensboro, NC 27425 USA

Author: Theresa Kane McKell
Illustrations: Don O'Connor

Printed in the USA • All rights reserved.
11 12 13 14 PAH 13 12 11 10

ISBN 978-0-7682-0260-1
214108091

Introduction

Algebra plays an important part in students' understanding of all mathematical concepts. Algebra organizes all operations that students perform. It is essential that students develop, understand, and learn to apply basic algebraic skills.

What is a variable?

How will algebra make me better understand how to compute rates, cost, and profit?

How are square roots and quadratic equations related?

How is exponential growth determined?

Students need to find answers to these and many other related questions in order to gain an understanding of all algebraic concepts.

Algebra Made Simple is the perfect opportunity to make algebra fun, relevant, and interesting for any student. It has been written to aid students in the development of a basic understanding of algebraic concepts and to help them learn and practice the skills necessary for this type of understanding. It contains activities that have been designed to provide students with a fun and exciting way to learn algebra and to give them a variety of everyday applications.

The objective of *Algebra Made Simple* is to give all students the opportunity to experience success in algebra. To help ensure this success, a wonderful variety of activities have been included and encompass a variety of different puzzles—some relating to real-life records, dates, and facts; others featuring riddlelike situations.

This book is divided into nine sections. At the beginning of each section are teacher resource pages. These pages contain many related activities and problems that can be used to guide students through each section. One exciting aspect of these resource pages is the Chapter Group Projects. These provide a fun way to help students work together to apply the concepts and skills presented in the section in order to create steps to solve a particular situation. These group activities give students the opportunity to see real-life applications of math in the world around them.

Following each set of teacher resource pages are interesting and exciting student activity pages. Students can work these pages to practice their skills and gain a conceptual understanding of the topics in each particular section. Some of the activities involve students in working puzzles, solving riddles, and decoding messages. And while the primary focus of each activity is the featured algebra skill, students will also enjoy the many jokes, record breakers, and riddles included.

The concepts covered in *Algebra Made Simple* are basic to most Algebra I courses. Students will develop a conceptual understanding of algebraic topics and will practice skills relating to the following specific concepts: real number system, solutions and graphs of linear equations, the writing of linear equations, calculation of absolute values and inequalities, solutions and graphs of linear systems, exponents, solutions to square roots and quadratic equations, and polynomials.

Algebra Made Simple is an easy and fun way to develop students' interest in and understanding of valuable algebraic concepts. You will be excited to observe as your students discover how stimulating learning algebra can be!

Working With Real Numbers

very algebra student will greatly benefit from the activities involving real numbers in this section. Allow
udents ample opportunity to work with
anipulatives and time to complete several
xamples with your guidance. Be sure students
ain a conceptual understanding of the concepts
 the right before proceeding through the
dependent student activity pages (pages 3–8).

resent everyday situations to students in
hich they may use their new skills. For
xample, students can use their knowledge of
al numbers as they balance a checkbook or
ompute automobile rental rates. Help students
oserve the world in which they live and
dentify their own connections involving real
umbers.

CONCEPTS

The ideas and activities presented in this section
will help students explore the following concepts:

- order of operations
- adding real numbers
- subtracting real numbers
- multiplying real numbers
- using the distributive property
- dividing real numbers

GETTING STARTED

o introduce the real number system, tell students to pretend that the only numbers they may use are {1,
 3, 4, 5, 6, 7, 8, . . .}. In groups, have them give examples of several different situations that cannot be
xplained by these numbers (when describing subzero temperatures—negative numbers; when using some
easurements in cooking—rational numbers; when using scientific notation). The students should then give
xamples of the numbers needed to describe these situations. To conclude this activity, students should give
everal examples of any other numbers they may use outside of school.

QUICK MOTIVATORS

- Ask students how gaining 15 yards in a football game
  can be related to losing 15 yards in a game.

- Ask students to explain when a good time would be to
  use a number line to add or subtract numbers. When
  would it most likely be impractical to use a number line
  when adding or subtracting?

- Ask students to define the relationship between addition
  and multiplication of real numbers. Students must
  give several examples. Show the difference between
  multiplying by a fraction and multiplying by a whole
  number, pointing out to them that multiplying by a whole
  number is simply repeated addition.

- Ask students to explain the relationship between
  multiplication and division. Show them several examples
  and have them give several examples.

FUN WITH MATH

Put the problems below on the board to get students on track and into algebra.

- Insert parentheses, where needed, in each of the expressions below so that each has the same value.

$$5 + 3 \times 2 \qquad 6 - 1 \times 2 + 12 \qquad 9 + 12 \div 3 + 3 \qquad 10 \div 2 + 3 + 14$$

Answers: $(5 + 3) \times 2 \qquad 6 - (1 \times 2) + 12 \qquad 9 + (12 \div 3) + 3 \qquad 10 \div (2 + 3) + 14$

- Replace each blank below with $+$, $-$, $\div$, or $\times$ to find the greatest value of the expression.

$$2 \_\_ 4 \_\_ 6 \_\_ 8 \_\_ 10 \_\_ 12 \quad \text{(Answer: } 2 \times 4 \times 6 \times 8 \times 10 \times 12)$$

- Use all five of the numbers 0, 2, 4, 6, 8 with any arithmetic operation, parentheses, and/or exponents to obtain the solutions of 0, 1, and 2. You must use each number exactly once!

Answers: $(2 \times 4) - 8 + (6 \times 0) = 0 \qquad 8 - 6 - 2 + 4^0 = 1 \qquad 0 \times (6 + 8) + 4 - 2 = 2$

EXPLORING EXTENSIONS

- Ask students to analyze the sums of $^-2 + (^-2) = ^-4$ and $^-2 + (^-2) + (^-2) = ^-6$.

  Have them use these patterns to simplify $^-2a + (^-2a)$ and $^-2a + (^-2a) + (^-2a)$. Students should describe their explanations in words.

- Ask students to analyze the sums of $^-3 + (^-4) = ^-7$ and $^-3 + (^-4) + (^-5) = ^-12$.

  Have them use these patterns to simplify $^-3a + (^-4a)$ and $^-3a + (^-4a) + (^-5a)$. Students should describe their explanations in words.

- Have students multiply each matrix by the whole number located outside its matrix.

$$^-2 \begin{bmatrix} ^-4 & 3 \\ 5 & ^-7 \end{bmatrix} \qquad 8 \begin{bmatrix} ^-5 & 7 \\ ^-3 & ^-1 \end{bmatrix} \qquad 10 \begin{bmatrix} 5 & ^-4 \\ ^-6 & 4 \end{bmatrix} \qquad 0 \begin{bmatrix} ^-4 & 10 \\ ^-2 & 9 \end{bmatrix}$$

Answers: $\begin{bmatrix} 8 & ^-6 \\ ^-10 & 14 \end{bmatrix} \begin{bmatrix} ^-40 & 56 \\ ^-24 & ^-8 \end{bmatrix} \begin{bmatrix} 50 & ^-40 \\ ^-60 & 40 \end{bmatrix} \begin{bmatrix} 0 & 0 \\ 0 & 0 \end{bmatrix}$

- Have students multiply each matrix, using the distributive property, by the whole number located outside the matrix.

$$^-3 \left(\begin{bmatrix} 5 & 4 \\ ^-7 & ^-8 \end{bmatrix} + \begin{bmatrix} ^-5 & 9 \\ 7 & ^-2 \end{bmatrix} \right) \qquad 8 \left(\begin{bmatrix} ^-2 & ^-1 \\ ^-8 & 10 \end{bmatrix} - \begin{bmatrix} ^-4 & 11 \\ 9 & ^-6 \end{bmatrix} \right)$$

Answers: $\begin{bmatrix} 0 & ^-39 \\ 0 & 30 \end{bmatrix} \qquad \begin{bmatrix} 16 & ^-96 \\ 136 & 128 \end{bmatrix}$

DEMONSTRATING MATH IDEAS

- Have students show how to model the sum of $^-6$ and $^-8$ two different ways.

- Ask students to describe the different ways the sum of $^-2$, $^-7$, 5, and $^-10$ can be modeled.

Chapter Group Project

Divide students into groups of three. Have each group explore the three methods of subtraction: (1) Decomposition Method, (2) Equal Addends Method, and (3) Addition of Nines Complements Method. Each student in each group will investigate and research one of the three methods. Once the research has been completed, each group should meet together to explain each member's method to the rest of the group. Once each member of the group knows all three methods, each can prepare a written report explaining in detail the three methods of subtraction. Or, the students could prepare a presentation describing in detail the process they used to explore these methods and what exactly they obtained.

Skipping Stones

Have you ever tried to skip stones across water? How many skips do you think holds the world record?

To find out, solve each problem. Shade in the boxes that contain your solutions. Read across the remaining unshaded boxes to spell out the answer.

1. $24 - 6 \div 2$

2. $(9 - 3) \times 5 \div 6$

3. $45 \div 15 + (2^3 \times 3)$

4. $9 - 3 + 28 \div 2^2$

5. $63 \div (4 \times 3 - 3)$

6. $30 \times 3 + 13 - 3$

7. $98 - [80 \div (20 - 16)]$

8. $4^2 \div (8 - 2^2) + 50$

9. $12 \times 12 + 144 \div 12 - 12$

10. $15 + 5 - 14 \div 7$

U	T	O	P	H	B	L
13	51	78	100	14	54	5
I	W	R	M	T	Y	S
44	18	62	27	75	105	144
E	D	I	G	N	H	T
9	7	12	22	21	63	0

Answer: _____

Math-a-Mania

If you were kidding around with a mathematician, what kind of jokes would this person play?

To find out, solve each expression. Write the letter of the corresponding problem above the given answer at the bottom of the page.

A. $6 + (^-12) + 5$

B. $^-13 + (^-2.1) + (^-3.3)$

C. $^-15 + 5 + (^-6)$

D. $52 + (^-42) + (^-10)$

E. $^-[14 + (^-8)]$

H. $7.5 + 4.5 + (^-7.5)$

I. $11 + (^-18) + 5$

K. $14.3 + (^-11.4)$

L. $^-(11 + 19)$

M. $(^-4) + (^-12) + (^-17)$

N. $3 + (^-7) + 4$

O. $^-[(^-5) + (^-5)]$

P. $6.8 + 8.3 + (^-13.1)$

R. $20 + (^-40) + (^-20)$

S. $0 + (^-21)$

T. $4.5 + (^-8.5) + (^-2.5)$

| $^-1$ | $^-40$ | $^-2$ | $^-6.5$ | 4.5 | $^-33$ | $^-6$ | $^-6.5$ | $^-40$ | $^-2$ | $^-16$ | 2.9 | $^-21$ |

State of Subtraction

Connecticut was the first state to have one of these in the United States. What was it that Connecticut had?

To find out, solve each expression. Write the letter that represents each answer in Column B next to each expression. Read down the column of written letters to discover the answer.

Column A

_____ **1.** ⁻4 – (⁻7)

_____ **2.** ⁻12 – (⁻3)

_____ **3.** 5 – (⁻8) – 1

_____ **4.** 9 – 13

_____ **5.** 83 – 91

_____ **6.** 4 – 32 – 8 – 34

_____ **7.** 20 – 36

_____ **8.** ⁻110 – (⁻10) – 50

_____ **9.** ⁻14 – 5

_____ **10.** ⁻80 – (⁻40)

_____ **11.** ⁻3 – 4 – 5

_____ **12.** ⁻4 – (⁻3) – 6

_____ **13.** ⁻6.7 – 6.7 – (⁻6.7)

_____ **14.** ⁻42 – 8 – (⁻24)

_____ **15.** 4.5 – 5.5 – 21

_____ **16.** 8.1 – 10.1 – 2.1 – (⁻4.1)

_____ **17.** 26 – 39 – (⁻26)

_____ **18.** ⁻5.1 – 6.1 – 2.8 – (⁻15)

_____ **19.** 108 – 110 – 18 – (⁻40)

Column B

E. ⁻70

C. ⁻150

W. 3

S. ⁻12

T. ⁻26

I. 12

T. 0

N. 20

T. ⁻8

O. ⁻19

T. ⁻7

O. 1

R. ⁻9

I. ⁻6.7

N. ⁻16

I. 13

N. ⁻40

U. ⁻22

T. ⁻4

Answer: _____

The Jazzy Jacksons

**These brothers were known as the Jackson Five.
Can you come up with all five of their first names?**

To find out their names, solve each problem. Write the problem number in front of the corresponding answer listed in the table. To spell out the answers at the bottom of the page, refer to the table and write the code letter that corresponds to the problem number given.

1. $(^-7)(^-8)$

2. $|(^-5)|(^-20)$

3. $(3)(^-1)|(^-11)|$

4. $(^-8)|(^-90)|$

5. $(^-7)(^-3a)(2)$

6. $(5)(7a)(^-2)$

7. $(26)(^-1)(^-3)(^-2)$

8. $|(4a)|(^-100)$

9. $(^-95)(^-2)(0)(^-5)$

10. $|(^-32)(4)|$

11. $(8a)(^-4)(^-1)$

12. $|(^-4)(^-2)(^-12)|$

13. $(^-5)|(15)|$

14. $(^-4)(^-6)(^-3a)$

15. $(^-9)|(^-10)(5)|$

Code Letter	Problem #	Answer
A		$^-33$
C		$^-156$
E		$32a$
H		$^-100$
I		$^-75$
J		^-400a
K		56
L		128
M		$42a$
N		96
O		0
R		$^-720$
T		^-70a
U		$^-450$
V		^-72a

___ ___ ___ ___ ___ ___ ___ ,   ___ ___ ___ ___ ___ ___ ,
 5   13   7   2   3   11   10   8   3   7   1   13   11

___ ___ ___ ___ ___ ___ ,   ___ ___ ___ ___ ___ ___ ___ ,
 5   3   4   10   9   12   8   11   4   5   3   13   12   11

and ___ ___ ___ ___
     6   13   6   9

FS122010 Algebra Made Simple ▪ © Carson-Dellosa

Shapin' Up

How well do you know your geometric shapes? Find out by testing your knowledge on the challenging "shaper-uppers" below.

Use the distributive property to determine if the left side of each equation is equal to the right. If both sides of the equation are equal, the corresponding statement is true; if both sides are not equal, the statement is false. If a statement is false, use your geometric knowledge to make it true. Correct each incorrect distribution problem on the blank provided below each problem.

---

1. A rhombus is a quadrilateral with sides of equal length and angles of equal measure.

$$5(x - 7) = x - 35$$ **True** or **False**?

---

2. An isosceles triangle is a triangle with all sides and angles congruent.

$$(x - 3)(^-5) = {}^-5x - 15$$ **True** or **False**?

---

3. A regular octagon is a polygon with eight sides of equal length and eight angles of equal measure.

$$(12x - 6)(^-3) = {}^-36x + 18$$ **True** or **False**?

---

4. A sphere is a globe-shaped figure with every point on its surface equidistant from its center.

$$(14 + 8x)(7) = 98 + 56x$$ **True** or **False**?

---

5. A trapezoid is a polygon with only two sides parallel and two angles congruent.

$$(20 - 6x)(^-4) = {}^-80 - 24x$$ **True** or **False**?

Amazing Achievement

In June, 1994, Michael Kearney made the *Guinness Book of World Records* when he became the youngest graduate to obtain a Bachelor of Arts degree in anthropology from the University of South Alabama. How old was he?

To find out, solve the problems. Count the number of negative answers. Your total will equal the answer to this amazing record.

1. $16 \div 2$

2. $9 \div \frac{1}{3}$

3. $^-7 \div \frac{7}{5}$

4. $^-4 \div \frac{1}{6}$

5. $^-6x = 24$

6. $^-50 = 10x$

7. $48 = ^-8x$

8. $^-x = 3$

9. $^-28x = ^-7$

10. $^-\frac{1}{2}x = 15$

11. $12 = ^-\frac{1}{4}x$

12. $18 = \frac{1}{6}x$

13. $90 \div (^-15)$

14. $72 = ^-\frac{1}{2}x$

15. $^-5 \div (^-\frac{1}{10})$

Answer: _____

   FS122010 Algebra Made Simple ■ © Carson-Dello

Solving Linear Equations

Every algebra student will greatly benefit from the activities involving solving linear equations in this section. Allow students ample opportunity to work with manipulatives and time to complete several examples with your guidance. Be sure students gain a conceptual understanding of the concepts below before proceeding through the independent student activity pages (pages 11–15).

Present everyday situations to students in which they may use their new skills. For example, students can use their knowledge of solving linear equations to determine the amount of profit they can make on specific items above their cost, or in studying the effects of new elements on the environment. Help students observe the world in which they live and identify their own connections involving solving linear equations.

CONCEPTS

The ideas and activities presented in this section will help students explore the following concepts:

- combining like terms
- one-step equations
- two-step equations
- variables on both sides
- literal equations

GETTING STARTED

Ask students to solve the following problems in their heads:

$9x = 72$	$x + 5 = 10$	$x - 7 = 20$	$\frac{1}{2}x = 12$
$(x = 8)$	$(x = 5)$	$(x = 27)$	$(x = 24)$

Then have each student explain, through writing, the method(s) actually used to solve such equations. For example, in $9x = 72$, we know $x = 8$, but how did we get to that conclusion? We actually divided both sides of the equation by 9 to get the desired result.

QUICK MOTIVATORS

- Ask students to explain how a balance scale would be useful when solving equations. You want them to reach the conclusion that what is done to one side of an equation must also be done to the other side.

- Ask students to give several examples of when the properties of addition and subtraction could not be used in solving an equation. Also, have them give several examples of when the properties of multiplication and division could not be useful.

- Ask students to translate the following into an equation and solve: *Five times the weight (pounds) of a hamster is the same as the weight increased by eight.* (Answer: $5x = x + 8$; $x = 2$)

FUN WITH MATH

Put the problems below on the board to get students on track and into algebra.

- Find the sum of the first 100 positive multiples of three. $[3(1 + 2 + 3 \ldots + 100)]$ Find the sum of the first 100 positive even integers. $[2(1 + 2 + 3 \ldots + 100)]$ Find their difference. Is there an easier way to calculate this other than the long way? [yes—$1 + 2 + 3 \ldots + 100 = 5050$]

- The local candy store is having a sale on candy bars. The prices are listed as follows:

  You can purchase a Snickers™ and a Heath™ bar for $.50.

  You can purchase a Heath™ and a Mars™ bar for $.75.

  You can purchase a Mars™ and a Twix™ bar for $.90.

  You can purchase a Twix™ and a Hershey™ bar for $1.00.

  You can purchase a Hershey™ and a Snickers™ bar for $.65.

  Determine the cost of each individual candy bar. Round to the nearest cent.

  (Answer: Snickers™ = $.15, Heath™ = $.35, Mars™ = $.40, Twix™ = $.50, Hershey™ = $.50)

EXPLORING EXTENSIONS

- Ask students to draw parallelogram MATH and label side MA $4x$ and side AT $2x$. Ask them to find the length of its sides, given the perimeter is 180. (Answer: MA = 60, AT = 30)

- Ask students to identify whether the solution steps below are correct. If not, have them explain the error(s) and write the correct set of steps to give the solution.

$$^-8x - 12 = 14 + 5x$$
$$8x - 5x - 12 = 14 - 14 + 5x - 5x$$
$$3x - 12 + 12 = 0 - 12$$
$$3x = ^-12$$
$$x = ^-4$$

Correct:
$$^-8x - 12 = 14 + 5x$$
$$^-8x - 5x - 12 = 14 + 5x - 5x$$
$$^-13x - 12 + 12 = 14 + 12$$
$$^-13x = 26$$
$$x = ^-2$$

DEMONSTRATING MATH IDEAS

- Ask students to write the steps they would use to solve $^-4x + 6 = 10x - 22$. With each step, have them give an explanation of why and how it was used. Then ask them to check their answers through substitution. (Answer: $x = 2$)

- Ask students to solve the problem below two ways, starting with a different step each time. Have them explain which process was easier and why. (Answer: $x = 7$)

$$7x - (4x - 7) = ^-14 + 6x$$

Chapter Group Project

This project can be worked in cooperative groups or independently. Ask students to pretend that each of them has been offered one of two different scholarships to go to college. Under the first scholarship, each would receive one-half of all college expenses. Under the second, $35,000 would be given for all expenses. Have the students suppose, also, that their parents have set aside $29,000 in a college fund for them. Have them suppose the fees to attend a state university for one year are $10,000, and for one year at a private institution, the fees are $20,000.

Ask students to write an equation to represent the cost for attending the state university for four years, and another equation representing the four-year cost of attending the private university. Ask students to give a detailed explanation of which university, state or private, they should attend and which scholarship they should receive. Be sure to have them explain why and give ample reasoning.

FS122010 Algebra Made Simple ▪ © Carson-Dellosa

Compromising Computers

How did all the computers afford to take a vacation?

To find out, solve the problems below in numerical order. Find the solutions in the box provided. Use the corresponding letters to spell out the answer. (Hint: There are four words in the answer.)

1. $17x - 5x$

2. $3x + 10x - 5x$

3. $26x - 14x + x$

4. $7x + 20x + 7x - 9x$

5. $11x + 75x - 20x$

6. $25x - 15x - 5x$

7. $100x - 90x - 9x$

8. $^-9(2x - 3x)$

9. $^-4(3x + 6y) + 12x + 4y$

10. $8(4x - 5y) + 9x$

11. $^-(^-5x + 7y) + 9(2x - 3y)$

12. $2(x + y) + x + y$

13. $10(x - 4y) + 5(^-6x + 3y)$

14. $^-7(5x - y) - 2y$

15. $^-(x - 8y) - (x + 9y)$

16. $3(^-3x - 4y) - 5(^-7x - y)$

H $= {}^-20y$	**P** $= 3x + 3y$	**L** $= x$	**P** $= 23x - 34y$
A $= 66x$	**I** $= 41x - 40y$	**C** $= 9x$	**L** $= 5x$
D $= {}^-35x + 5y$	**N** $= 26x - 7y$	**E** $= {}^-20x - 25y$	**I** $= {}^-2x - y$
T $= 12x$	**E** $= 13x$	**H** $= 8x$	**Y** $= 25x$

Answer: _____

Merry Multiplication

Can you imagine having to multiply two enormously large numbers without using a calculator? At Imperial College in London, England, on June 18, 1980, Shakuntala Devi multiplied two randomly selected 13-digit numbers (7,686,369,774,870 x 2,465,099,745,779). Her answer, which was found to be correct, was 18,947,668,177,995,426,462,773,730. How many seconds did this multiplication feat take?

To find out, solve the problems below. Circle the letters that represent the solutions. To spell out the answer to the question, copy each circled letter onto the line that is labeled with its corresponding problem number.

1. $x + 5 = 3$

2. $7x = 21$

3. $40 = x + 43$

4. $x \div 8 = {}^-1$

5. $9 + x = {}^-2$

6. $12x = 48$

7. $8 + x = {}^-20$

8. $x \div {}^-2 = {}^-8$

9. ${}^-102 = 51x$

10. $x - 19 = {}^-20$

11. $35 + x = {}^-6$

Y. 4

G. ⁻2

T. 2

N. ⁻8

T. ⁻41

E. ⁻28

W. 3

I. 16

T. ⁻11

E. ⁻3

H. ⁻1

___ ___ ___ ___ ___ ___   ___   ___ ___ ___ ___ ___
 1   2   3   4   5   6   7   8   9   10   11

Art Alert

How big is the largest painting you have ever seen? The record for the largest painting in the world is 76,726 square feet found on the island of Tybee, Georgia. It was painted by some students at the Savannah College of Art and Design. What famous person is this a painting of?

To find out, solve each equation for x. Compare the answers of each pair and circle the letter of the one with the greater value. Write the circled letters in problem order to spell out the name of the person in this awesome painting.

1. (G) $\frac{1}{4}x + 10 = 2$
   (E) $\frac{1}{3}x + 8 = 4$

2. (A) $\frac{1}{5}x + 3 = 5$
   (L) $10 + \frac{1}{7}x = 12$

3. (V) $13 + \frac{1}{2}x = 15$
   (R) $\frac{1}{6}x - 4 = {}^-6$

4. (I) $8 - \frac{1}{7}x = 9$
   (O) $\frac{1}{3}x + 5 = {}^-1$

5. (S) $2x - 4 = 16$
   (T) $4x - 10 = {}^-30$

6. (F) $12x + 2 = 26$
   (P) $^-4x - 12 = {}^-36$

7. (Y) $20 = 8x - 4$
   (R) $9 = 3x - 3$

8. (A) $6x - 1 = 17$
   (E) $11x - 54 = 1$

9. (S) $110 - 10x = 10$
   (M) $4x - 3 = 33$

10. (B) $14x + 3 = {}^-25$
    (L) $30 = 5x - 15$

11. (I) $^-25 = 10x - 5$
    (E) $28 = 7x + 28$

12. (Y) $9x + 40 = {}^-14$
    (R) $20x + 41 = {}^-199$

Answer: _____

Mighty Small

This state is the smallest state in the United States. However, it contains more people to the square mile than any state except New Jersey. What is the name of this small, but mighty, state?

To find out, solve each problem. Shade in the boxes that contain the solutions. Read across the remaining unshaded boxes to spell out the answer.

1. $4x = 12x + 32$

2. $25x + 30 = 15x$

3. $^-30x = ^-180 + 30x$

4. $^-3(x + 2) = 16 - x$

5. $28 + 12x = 8x - 4$

6. $5(x - 2) = (x + 6)$

7. $60x + 153 = 9x + 51$

8. $^-x - 2(9 - 8x) = 12$

9. $^-4x - 10 = ^-5x + 18$

10. $6(x - 6) = x(16 - 7)$

R	T	I	H	O	Y	D
0	4	28	-7	6	-4	10
N	B	E	I	V	R	S
3	2	-5	-9	-11	-3	13
L	H	A	C	N	W	D
11	-8	-14	-2	9	-12	-10

Answer: _____

FS122010 Algebra Made Simple ▪ © Carson-Dellos

Sportin' Up

> **If the basketball team at your school was chasing the baseball team, what time would it be?**

To find out, solve the equations below for y in terms of x. Find the letter in Column B representing the answer to its problem in Column A. Write the letter in front of its problem number. Read down the column of written letters to discover the answer to the riddle.

Column A

_____ 1. $x + y = 4$

_____ 2. $y - x = {}^-3$

_____ 3. $x - y = {}^-1$

_____ 4. $4x + y = 10$

_____ 5. $6x + y = {}^-12$

_____ 6. $8x - y = {}^-7$

_____ 7. $^-2x + y = 9$

_____ 8. $^-y + 3x = {}^-11$

_____ 9. $13x - y = 4$

_____ 10. $2y + 4x = 6$

_____ 11. $9x - 3y = 12$

_____ 12. $2y - 6x = 8$

_____ 13. $^-x - y = {}^-1$

Column B

T. $y = 2x + 9$

V. $y = x + 1$

W. $y = 4x + 10$

A. $y = {}^-6x - 12$

F. $y = {}^-x + 4$

N. $y = 3x + 4$

R. $y = 13x - 4$

M. $y = {}^-13x - 4$

E. $y = {}^-x + 1$

I. $y = x - 3$

L. $y = 8x - 7$

F. $y = 8x + 7$

E. $y = {}^-4x + 10$

N. $y = {}^-2x + 3$

E. $y = 3x + 11$

I. $y = 3x - 4$

Answer: _____

Graphing Linear Equations

Every algebra student will greatly benefit from the activities involving graphing linear equations in this section. Allow students ample opportunity to work with manipulatives and time to complete several examples with your guidance. Be sure students gain a conceptual understanding of the concepts to the right before proceeding through the independent student activity pages (pages 18–26).

Present everyday situations to students in which they may use their new skills. For example, students can use their knowledge of graphing linear equations to visualize relationships between two variables in the areas of weather, business, school, and many other related fields. Help students observe the world in which they live and identify their own connections involving graphing linear equations.

CONCEPTS

The ideas and activities presented in this section will help students explore the following concepts:

- one-variable graphs
- two-variable graphs
- graphing x- and y-intercepts
- slope of a line
- classifying slopes
- graphing slopes
- slope-intercept form
- graphing slopes and y-intercepts

GETTING STARTED

Ask students to give you the definitions and some of the uses of the words below. Be sure they do not use dictionaries. You want this to be off the top of their heads.

slope   coordinate   intercept   rise   run   line

When you have finished discussing these words and the students' definitions, help students formulate the relationship of these words to each other and to the world of math and graphing.

QUICK MOTIVATORS

- Ask students to give several examples of when knowing the slope is needed or could be helpful. For example, the slope of a road can help someone gauge the speed to travel.

- Show students the graph of $y = 4x$, marking several points along with their coordinates. Then have students figure the slope using at least three different sets of points on the line. Ask students to draw a conclusion based on the information given and the results acquired. Be sure they give a thorough explanation.

FS122010 Algebra Made Simple ▪ © Carson-Dellosa

FUN WITH MATH

Put the problems below on the board to get students on track and into algebra.

- Find the area of a rectangle whose vertices are (0, 3), (4, 3), (0, ⁻2), and (4, ⁻2). In order to visualize the actual rectangle, plot the points on a graph and connect the dots. (Answer: 20 square units)

- Given the graph of a line to the right and two points on the line, name the following points on the line only given one of the coordinates of each: (5, __), (__, 10). [Answer: (5, 6), (7, 10)]

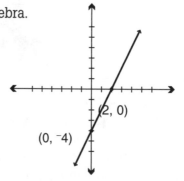

(2, 0)

(0, ⁻4)

EXPLORING EXTENSIONS

- Ask students to plot each of the tables of values below on separate graphs. Ask them to describe the relationship between x and y in both tables. Then ask them to write the equation representing each relationship, which will actually be the equation of the line represented in each table.

Table #1

x	0	1	2	3	4	5	6	7	8
y	1	2	3	4	5	6	7	8	9

(x and y values both increase as the other increases; $y = x + 1$)

Table #2

x	0	1	2	3	4	5	6	7	8
y	2	1	0	⁻1	⁻2	⁻3	⁻4	⁻5	⁻6

(as x increases, y decreases; $y = ⁻x + 2$)

- Ask students to find the value of y so that the line passing through (4, 5) and (6, y) will have a slope of $\frac{5}{2}$. (Answer: $y = 10$)

DEMONSTRATING MATH IDEAS

Ask students to make an educated guess about how many students were in your high school in the years 1990 through your current year. Have them create a chart with the years, ranging from 1990 to 2000, and the number of assumed graduates in each of those years. Then they can graph the actual data on the same coordinate plane, labeling the x-axis with the years and the y-axis with the number of estimated graduates. Students use their graphs to estimate the number of graduates in the year 2000 and beyond. Be sure your students can give ample explanation of their estimations.

Chapter Group Project

Divide students into groups of three to conduct a sports survey. Each person in the group should randomly select 15 people, varying in age, to determine their sports preference. Some ideas of different sports could be soccer, baseball, volleyball, basketball, tennis, football, wrestling, and swimming.

Ask students to combine their results and compare them to the others in their group. Have them give detailed explanations of how their results differ or are comparable. Have each student create a bar graph to show the results for each type of sport. Ask students what the five most popular sports were and the age distribution of those people selected for the survey. Ask students to compare the male and female sports preferences in relation to the age groups by creating a line graph. Have students compare their graphs and come up with their conclusions using the detailed information gathered.

Way-Out Wealth

If you were extremely wealthy, what would the air that you breathe be called?

To find out, graph each $x = a$ equation on the large graph below. Write next to each graphed line the letter associated with the equation. Read the letters on the grid from left to right to discover the first part of the riddle's answer. Repeat the process with each $y = b$ graph, reading downward to reveal the second part of the answer.

I. $x = {}^-4$ **I.** $y = 2$

L. $x = 3$ **L.** $x = 1$

R. $y = {}^-3$ **O.** $x = 6$

I. $x = 4$ **A.** $y = 5$

N. $x = 7$ **M.** $x = {}^-6$

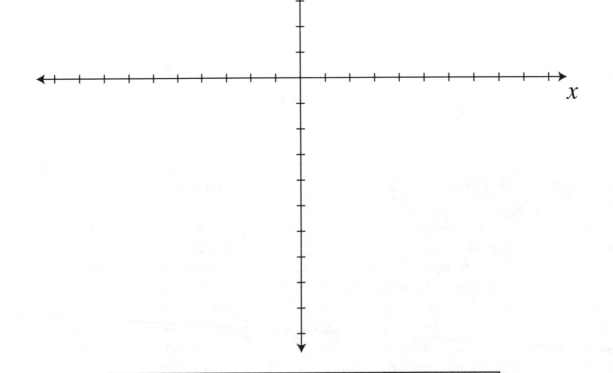

Answer: _____

FS122010 Algebra Made Simple ▪ © Carson-Dellosa

Mac-Attack

This corporation is the largest food service retailer in the world. At the end of 1996, it operated 21,022 restaurants in 101 countries around the world. Worldwide sales in 1996 were nearly $31.8 billion. What is the name of this famous food chain?

To find out, circle the coordinate pair that is a solution to each equation. The letter next to the solution will spell out the answer to the trivia question.

1.	$y = 3x + 6$	**J** $(4, {}^-18)$		**M** $({}^-3, {}^-3)$
2.	$y = {}^-x - 7$	**C** $(1, {}^-8)$		**A** $(0, 7)$
3.	$y = 8x + 5$	**D** $({}^-1, {}^-3)$		**C** $({}^-2, 4)$
4.	$y = {}^-4x - 3$	**K** $(2, 5)$		**O** $({}^-1, 1)$
5.	$y = {}^-3x + 8$	**I** $({}^-2, 2)$		**N** $(1, 5)$
6.	$2x + 8y = 6$	**N** $(0, {}^-3)$		**A** $({}^-5, 2)$
7.	$x + 4y = {}^-3$	**B** $({}^-1, 2)$		**L** $(1, {}^-1)$
8.	${}^-x - y = 12$	**D** $({}^-5, {}^-7)$		**O** $(5, 7)$
9.	$2x - 5y = {}^-4$	**X** $(8, {}^-4)$		**S** $(8, 4)$

Answer: _____ Corporation

Name

Bursting With Bubbles

The longest one of these bubbles ever blown was 105 feet long. Alan McKay of Wellington, New Zealand, created this using a bubble wand. What kind of bubble was this great creation?

To find out, determine the coordinate points for each equation by completing a "table of values" for x and y. Use the values to help identify the graph of each equation. Match each equation to its corresponding graph. Write the corresponding letter above the problem number.

1. $y = x - 3$

2. $y = x + 2$

3. $y = {}^-x + 6$

4. $y = {}^-3x + 4$

5. $y = x - 5$

6. $y = {}^-x + 4$

7. $y = 2x - 1$

8. $y = {}^-4x - 2$

9. $y = {}^-x - 1$

10. $y = {}^-4x + 2$

B.
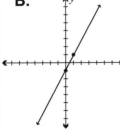

A.
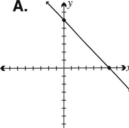

E.
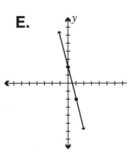

B.
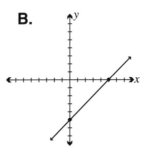

S.
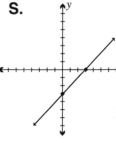

O.
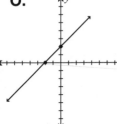

U.
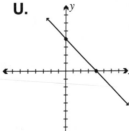

P.
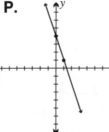

B.
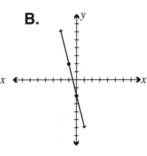

L.
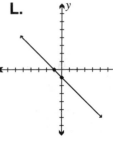

___ ___ ___ ___   ___ ___ ___ ___ ___ ___
 1   2   3   4   5   6   7   8   9   10

Fabulous Football

Doesn't finding the *x*- and *y*-intercepts make you think of interceptions in football? Paul Krause holds the record for the most interceptions in a football career. He played with the Washington Redskins and then for the Minnesota Vikings in the years 1964–1979. How many interceptions did he have?

To find out, determine the *x*- and *y*-intercept of each equation. At the bottom of the page, write the letter of each problem above its solution to decode the answer.

E. $-8x + 2y = 32$

I. $-10x - 3y = 30$ **G.** $-6x - 4y = 48$

H. $3x + 5y = 15$ **Y.** $13x - 13y = -26$ **T.** $7x - 3y = -21$

O. $6x - 14y = 42$ **N.** $9x - 15y = 45$

E. $-2x + 4y = -16$

$x = -4$	$x = -3$	$x = -8$	$x = 5$	$x = -3$	$x = -2$		$x = 7$	$x = 5$	$x = 8$
$y = 16$	$y = -10$	$y = -12$	$y = 3$	$y = 7$	$y = 2$		$y = -3$	$y = -3$	$y = -4$

School Silly

If you were a thermometer, why would you have to go to school?

To find out, use the points given in each problem below to find the slope of the line passing through each set of points. Write the problem number in front of its corresponding slope listed in the table. To spell out the answer at the bottom of the page, refer to the table and write the code letter that corresponds to the problem number given.

1. (3, 4), (5, 8)

2. (1, 0), (0, ⁻1)

3. (9, 5), (11, ⁻3)

4. (3, 3), (2, ⁻2)

5. (⁻7, 4), (6, ⁻9)

6. (5, ⁻6), (8, ⁻6)

7. (10, 1), (12, 7)

8. (⁻7, 5), (⁻5, ⁻7)

9. (⁻1, 6), (⁻1, ⁻11)

10. (8, ⁻3), (7, 4)

11. (⁻13, ⁻2), (⁻10, 10)

12. (0, ⁻5), (⁻4, 3)

13. (9, 1), (10, 8)

Code Letter	Problem #	Answer
A		3
D		1
E		⁻7
G		⁻1
H		2
I		undefined
N		0
O		⁻4
R		4
S		⁻6
T		5
U		7
Y		⁻2

___ ___   ___ ___ ___ ___   ___ ___ ___ ___
 4   3   10   7 11   6   12   3 13 11

___ ___ ___ ___ ___ ___ ___ **!**
 2 10   5 11 10 10   8

FS122010 Algebra Made Simple ▪ © Carson-Dellosa

Pancake Pacing

Could you ever imagine running in a marathon while flipping a pancake? Believe it or not, Dominic Cuzzacrea made the Guinness Book of World Records with the fastest time in finishing the Buffalo Nissan Marathon while flipping a pancake on May 6, 1990. Just how fast did she complete this marathon?

To find out, find the slope of the line for each pair of points. Write in the blank next to each problem number whether the line is vertical, horizontal, rising from left to right, or falling from left to right. Count the number of problems that contain the answer of rising from left to right—this will be the number of hours it took to complete the marathon. Count the number of problems that contain the answer of falling from left to right—this will be the remaining minutes of the official time.

_____ 1. (5, 4), (9, ⁻8)   slope = _____

_____ 2. (0, ⁻1), (2, ⁻3)   slope = _____

_____ 3. (3, ⁻3), (6, 6)   slope = _____

_____ 4. (⁻10, 2), (⁻10, ⁻2)   slope = _____

_____ 5. (⁻5, 6), (2, ⁻8)   slope = _____

_____ 6. (0, 4), (⁻3, ⁻14)   slope = _____

_____ 7. (⁻7, ⁻3), (9, ⁻3)   slope = _____

_____ 8. (2, ⁻5), (⁻1, 13)   slope = _____

_____ 9. (8, 0), (9, ⁻5)   slope = _____

_____ 10. (⁻9, 3), (⁻9, 0)   slope = _____

_____ 11. (⁻12, 2), (⁻10, 10)   slope = _____

_____ 12. (4, ⁻5), (⁻1, 15)   slope = _____

Answer: _____

Jumpin' Jellybeans

The Disney channel sponsored the largest jar of jellybeans ever recorded in the world in October 1992 at Westside Pavilion, Los Angeles, California. The jar contained 378,000 jellybeans and weighed a total of 2,910 pounds. How many inches tall was this jellybean jar?

To find out, graph the line that corresponds to the given values for each problem on a piece of graph paper. Circle the letter that describes the line. Unscramble the circled letters to spell out the answer.

1. $(3, 5)$, $m = 2$
    (E) line rises from left to right
    (R) line falls from left to right

2. $(^-2, 0)$, $m = ^-1$
    (G) horizontal line
    (N) line falls from left to right

3. $(^-3, 4)$, $m = 0$
    (S) horizontal line
    (H) line rises from left to right

4. $(6, ^-1)$, $m = ^-\frac{4}{5}$
    (T) vertical line
    (X) line falls from left to right

5. $(^-3, 0)$, $m = 4$
    (Y) line rises from left to right
    (C) line falls from left to right

6. $(^-5, ^-5)$, $m =$ undefined
    (M) horizontal line
    (I) vertical line

7. $(2, ^-1)$, $m = ^-\frac{1}{3}$
    (N) line falls from left to right
    (O) line rises from left to right

8. $(4, ^-2)$, $m = \frac{1}{4}$
    (W) vertical line
    (I) line rises from left to right

9. $(0, 3)$, $m = \frac{1}{2}$
    (T) line rises from left to right
    (H) horizontal line

Answer: _____

Feet-Finders

If you were a true mathematician, what kind of feet would you have?

To find out, change each equation below into the slope-intercept form ($y = mx + b$), and identify the slope (m) and the y-intercept (b). Circle the letters that represent the solutions. Copy each circled letter onto the line at the bottom of the page that is labeled with its corresponding problem number.

1. $x + y = 4$

2. $^-3x - y = 7$

3. $5x + y = 9$

4. $2x - 2y = 8$

5. $^-12x + 4y = 12$

6. $^-x - 2y = 6$

7. $x - y = 11$

8. $8x - 4y = 16$

9. $^-10x + 5y = ^-30$

10. $^-x + 3y = 15$

R. $y = 3x + 3$
   $m = 3, b = 3$

Q. $y = ^-3x - 7$
   $m = ^-3, b = ^-7$

F. $y = x - 11$
   $m = 1, b = ^-11$

E. $y = 2x - 6$
   $m = 2, b = ^-6$

S. $y = ^-x + 4$
   $m = ^-1, b = 4$

T. $y = \frac{1}{3}x + 5$
   $m = \frac{1}{3}, b = 5$

A. $y = x - 4$
   $m = 1, b = ^-4$

E. $y = ^-\frac{1}{2}x - 3$
   $m = ^-\frac{1}{2}, b = ^-3$

U. $y = ^-5x + 9$
   $m = ^-5, b = 9$

E. $y = 2x - 4$
   $m = 2, b = ^-4$

| 1 | 2 | 3 | 4 | 5 | 6 | | 7 | 8 | 9 | 10 |

Miles of Isles

Not counting Australia, which is usually considered a continental landmass, what is the largest island in the world, covering an area of about 840,000 square miles?

To find out, graph the equations below using the values for slope and *y*-intercept. Match each of your graphs with its graph below. Write the problem letter next to each graph. Read the letters by the graphs from left to right to identify the answer.

E. $y = -2x - 4$　　**R.** $y = -\frac{1}{2}x - 2$　　**E.** $y = -3x$　　**A.** $y = x$　　**N.** $y = \frac{1}{5}x + 2$

N. $y = x - 5$　　**L.** $y = -x$　　**G.** $y = \frac{3}{4}x - 1$　　**D.** $y = 4x + 3$

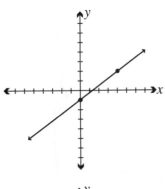
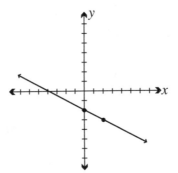
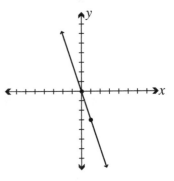

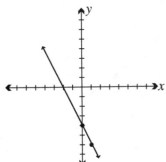
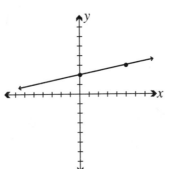
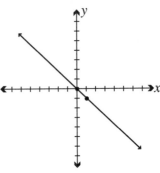

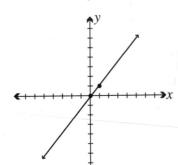
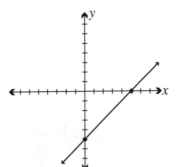
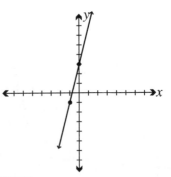

Answer: _____

Writing Linear Equations

Every algebra student will greatly benefit from the activities involving writing linear equations in this section. Allow students ample opportunity to work with manipulatives and time to complete several examples with your guidance. Be sure students gain a conceptual understanding of the concepts below before proceeding through the independent student activity pages (pages 29–35).

Present everyday situations to students in which they may use their new skills. For example, students can use their knowledge of writing linear equations to solve cost problems, to find the rate of change, and to buy several items with a fixed amount of money. Help students observe the world in which they live and identify their own connections involving writing linear equations.

CONCEPTS

The ideas and activities presented in this section will help students explore the following concepts:

- writing slope-intercept form
- using two points to write equations
- reading graphs and writing equations
- writing standard form of equations
- writing point-slope form of equations

GETTING STARTED

Ask students to solve the following equations for y:

$$2x + y = 6 \qquad\qquad 6x - 3y = {}^-12 \qquad\qquad {}^-x + 4y = 8$$
$$(y = {}^-2x + 6) \qquad\quad (y = 2x + 4) \qquad\qquad (y = \tfrac{1}{4}x + 2)$$

Once they have completed this, have them compare the two different forms of the same equation. What is the difference in $Ax + By = C$ and $y = mx + b$? Can they conclude more information with one equation than the other? Ask them if they know the name of each of these forms of linear equations. ($Ax + By = C$ is standard form, $y = mx + b$ is slope-intercept form.)

QUICK MOTIVATORS

- Ask students to graph the following points: M (1, 1), A (1, 6), T (6, 6), H (6, 1). Have students connect the dots. What shape do these connected points create? (square) Ask students to find the slopes of the segments MA, AT, TH, and HM. (MA = $\tfrac{5}{0}$, AT = $\tfrac{0}{5}$, TH = $\tfrac{{}^-5}{0}$, HM = $\tfrac{0}{{}^-5}$) How do the slopes of the parallel and perpendicular sides of the square relate? (negative reciprocals of each other) Ask them to thoroughly explain their conclusions using the information they found.

- Ask each student to find a partner. Have each student write two equations in slope-intercept form, standard form, or point-slope form, and graph them on a separate sheet of paper. Then have them exchange the graphs with their partners. Ask each student to write the equation of each partner's graphs. When the equations of the exchanged graphs are completed, ask the students to return the work to the original writer so that it can be checked for accuracy.

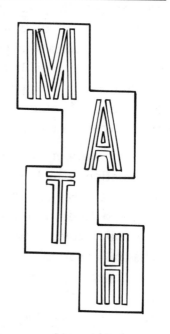

FUN WITH MATH

Put the problems below on the board to get students on track and into algebra.

- Have students imagine that they have a job in a bike shop. Their boss asks them to count the number of motorcycles and the number of 4-wheelers they have in stock. Rather than just doing exactly what the boss asked, your students decide to count the total number of wheels and the number of brakes (each vehicle having two brakes). They count 212 wheels and 180 brakes. Ask students to find the number of motorcycles and the number of 4-wheelers in the bike shop. (74 motorcycles, 16 4-wheelers)

- Have students imagine that their cat was being chased by a dog. A cat on a tree limb with a slope of -3 was spotted from a kitchen window located at $(2, 0)$. A cat on another tree limb with a slope of -2 was spotted by a fireman located at $(2, -3)$. What are the coordinates of the position of the cat? $(5, -9)$

Chapter Group Project

Divide students into groups of three. In this project, students will compare two swimming pools' admission policies. Have students imagine that there are two pools in your area: the public pool and a semi-private pool. The public pool charges an admission of $4.25 a day to use its pool. The semi-private pool requires a membership card, which costs $20 per year, and then a daily rate of $3.00 each time you visit. Which is the most economical pool to use for the summer? If you rarely go to the pool, which would be a better deal? If you go to the pool often, which would be better?

Have the students graph their information. Also, have them develop a linear equation for each pool to describe the amount of money it costs to swim at each. What other variables should be considered along with the cost? The students should describe their investigation in detail along with their conclusions.

EXPLORING EXTENSIONS

- Ask students to write an equation of the line that has the same slope as $y = -2x - 2$ and the same y-intercept as $y = \frac{1}{4}x + 3$. Have them graph all three lines. $(y = -2x + 3)$

- Ask students to determine whether the three points in each group below lie on the same line. If they do, have them find the equation of that line.

  a. $(4, 5)$, $(-2, 5)$, $(0, 5)$ (yes; $y = 5$)

  b. $(-1, 9)$, $(9, 3)$, $(4, 9)$ (no)

  c. $(7, -3)$, $(7, 2)$, $(7, -5)$ (yes; $x = 7$)

- Ask students to refer to this equation to answer the questions below: $2x + 9y = 18$.

  * What are the x- and y-intercepts of this graph? $(x = 9, y = 2)$

  * Multiply each term in the equation by $\frac{1}{18}$. $(\frac{1}{9}x + \frac{1}{2}y = 1$

  * For the equation obtained when multiplying by $\frac{1}{18}$, find how the denominators on the left side of this equation relate to the x- and y-intercepts. (They are the same values.)

  * Explain your reasoning on this relationship.

DEMONSTRATING MATH IDEAS

On the board, write: *The cost for tickets to the World's Fair is a flat fee of $50 for a group of 20 or more and $10 for each person in the group.* Ask students to write a linear model for the total cost of tickets for a group of 45. $(y = 10x + 50$; cost of a group of 45 is $500)

FS122010 Algebra Made Simple ▪ © Carson-Dello

Earth Shaking

What city in the United States had the most expensive destruction caused by any earthquake in U.S. history (close to $20 billion)? (Hint: It happened on January 17, 1994.)

To find out, write the equation of each line given its slope (*m*) and *y*-intercept (*b*). Shade in the boxes that contain your answers. Read across the remaining unshaded boxes to spell out the answer.

1. $m = 2, b = 5$

2. $m = {}^-1/2, b = 7$

3. $m = {}^-4, b = {}^-7$

4. $m = 0, b = 2$

5. $m = 1/2, b = {}^-3$

6. $m = 2, b = 0$

7. $m = {}^-5, b = 2$

8. $m = 7, b = 4$

9. $m = 1, b = {}^-2$

10. $m = {}^-1, b = {}^-1$

L	H	O	P	B
$y = x - 1$	$y = 2x + 5$	$y = {}^-7x - 4$	$y = 2$	$y = {}^-5x + 2$
N	S	A	Y	D
$y = {}^-1/2x + 7$	$y = {}^-2x$	$y = 1/2x + 3$	$y = {}^-x - 1$	$y = 2x$
N	C	G	E	A
$y = {}^-2x - 5$	$y = 7x + 4$	$y = 5x + 2$	$y = x + 2$	$y = 1/2x - 3$
L	E	R	T	S
$y = 2x + 7$	$y = 4x - 7$	$y = x - 2$	$y = {}^-4x - 7$	$y = {}^-x - 2$

Answer: _____

Double Doggy Dare

If a dog says "Barf, Barf!" when it gets sick, what is it going to say if it sits on sandpaper?

To find out, write the equation of each line given its slope (m) and one coordinate point. Circle the y-intercept value in each equation. To spell out the answer to the question, match the letter of each problem to the corresponding y-intercept value at the bottom of the page.

F. $(2, 0)$, $m = {}^{-}3$ **U.** $(0, {}^{-}5)$, $m = 2$ **R.** $(2, {}^{-}1)$, $m = 3$ **F.** $(5, {}^{-}6)$, $m = {}^{-}2$

R. $(4, 0)$, $m = {}^{-}\frac{3}{4}$ **F.** $(3, {}^{-}2)$, $m = 2$ **U.** $(3, 9)$, $m = \frac{4}{3}$ **F.** $(2, {}^{-}6)$, $m = {}^{-}3$

" __ __ __ __ , __ __ __ __ !"
    3   ⁻5   0   4   ⁻7   5   6   ⁻8

Shoe-Sational

Matthew McGrory of Pennsylvania, born in 1973, is known to hold the record for the biggest feet in the world. What size shoe does he wear?

To find out, write the equation of the line for each set of ordered pairs. Write the corresponding letters from Column A in front of the equations in Column B.

Column A

N. (0, 3), (−2, 6)

S. (4, −1), (1, 2)

W. (−1, 5), (2, −10)

Y. (3, −3), (2, −7)

X. (3, −4), (5, 2)

T. (10, −1), (9, −1)

E. (2, −4), (5, 5)

I. (6, 2), (4, 1)

T. (−2, −4), (1, 2)

Column B

_____ $y = 2x$

_____ $y = {}^-5x$

_____ $y = 3x - 10$

_____ $y = {}^-3/2x + 3$

_____ $y = {}^-1$

_____ $y = 4x - 15$

_____ $y = {}^-x + 3$

_____ $y = 1/2x - 1$

_____ $y = 3x - 13$

Answer: _____

Delicious Delight

The world's largest one of these was made with 2.8 tons of chocolate on April 2, 1996, in Christchurch, New Zealand. It had an area of 5,241.5 square feet and a diameter of 81 feet 8 inches. What was this monstrous delight we all love?

To find out, match each equation to its graph. (Hint: Compare slope and *y*-intercept values.) Write the letter representing the equation next to its graph. Read the letters from left to right to identify the name of this delight.

O. $y = {}^-3x - 1$

I. $y = 2x + 4$

K. $y = {}^-x + 3$

E. $y = \frac{1}{3}x - 1$

O. $y = {}^-2x - 4$

C. $y = x - 3$

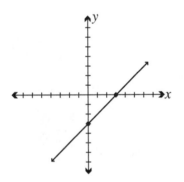

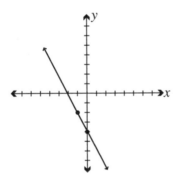

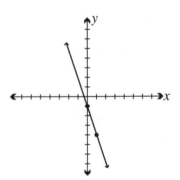

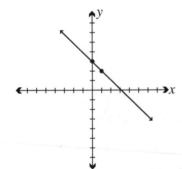

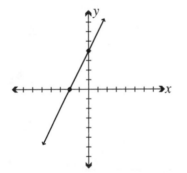

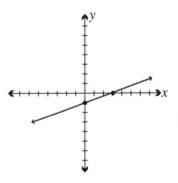

Answer: _____

FS122010 Algebra Made Simple ▪ © Carson-Dellos

ame

Happy Helpers

If you were one of Santa Claus' helpers, what would you be called?

To find out, write the standard form of each equation. Write the letter of the problem above its answer at the bottom of the page.

N. $y = {}^-4x + 4$

C. $y = {}^-x - 7$

S. $y = 6x + 3$

T. $y = 6x - 7$

D. $y = {}^-5x + 8$

A. $y = 8x + 11$

E. ${}^-4x - 3y - 10 = {}^-8$

N. $8x + 7y - 3 = 0$

E. $3x - y - 12 = {}^-20$

P. $9x - 5y = 13 - 7$

L. ${}^-4x - 4y - 4 = {}^-9$

E. ${}^-6x - 5y - 3 = 4$

U. ${}^-10x + 11y - 12 = {}^-10$

D. $3x - 7y - 8 + 3 = 13$

$\overline{}$ $\overline{}$ $\overline{}$ $\overline{}$ $\overline{}$ $\overline{}$ $\overline{}$ $\overline{}$ $\overline{}$
$3x - 7y = 18$ ${}^-6x - 5y = 7$ $9x - 5y = 6$ $3x - y = {}^-8$ $8x + 7y = 3$ $5x + y = 8$ ${}^-4x - 3y = 2$ $4x + y = 4$ ${}^-6x + y = {}^-7$

$\overline{}$ $\overline{}$ $\overline{}$ $\overline{}$ $\overline{}$
$x + y = {}^-7$ ${}^-4x - 4y = {}^-5$ ${}^-8x + y = 11$ ${}^-10x + 11y = 2$ ${}^-6x + y = 3$

Mathematics Minor

Colin Maclaurin is known to be the youngest professor that has ever lived in the world. He was elected to Marischal College, Aberdeen, Scotland, as Professor of Mathematics in 1717. How old was he?

To find out, write the equation of a line in standard form that includes the values given for each problem. Find the matching equation in the list to the right. Write the letter representing its solution in front of each problem number.

$(^-3x^2) (^-7x) (^-2x^4)$

$(^-12x) ($

_____ 1. $m = 2$, $b = 1$ **T.** $^-5/2x + y = 4$

_____ 2. $(3, 3)$, $m = 2$ **E.** $5x - y = 3$

_____ 3. $(7, ^-2)$, $(10, 1)$ **I.** $^-2x + y = ^-3$

_____ 4. $m = ^-4$, $b = 8$ **N.** $x + 3y = 3$

_____ 5. $(2, 9)$, $m = 5/2$ **N.** $^-x + y = ^-9$

_____ 6. $(2, ^-6)$, $(1, ^-2)$ **E.** $4x + y = 8$

_____ 7. $(^-1, ^-8)$, $m = 5$ **N.** $^-2x + y = 1$

_____ 8. $(6, ^-1)$, $(^-3, 2)$ **E.** $8x + 2y = 4$

Answer: _____

Raging River

What is the name of the longest river system in the United States, flowing 2,348 miles through 25 states?

To find out, write the equation of a line in point-slope form that includes the given values for each problem. Circle the letter in each problem that represents the equation of the line. To find the answer, write the corresponding letter above its problem number at the bottom of the page.

1. $(^-5, 4)$, $m = 6$
  (T) $y - 4 = 6(x + 5)$
  (K) $y + 4 = 6(^-x + 5)$

2. $(3, 2)$, $m = ^-2$
  (D) $y - 3 = ^-2(x - 2)$
  (H) $y - 2 = ^-2(x - 3)$

3. $(^-1, 4)$, $m = 5$
  (E) $y - 4 = 5(x + 1)$
  (R) $y + 4 = 5(x - 1)$

4. $(^-9, ^-6)$, $m = ^-3$
  (M) $y + 6 = ^-3(x + 9)$
  (N) $y + 9 = ^-3(x + 6)$

5. $(4, 0)$, $m = 7$
  (U) $y - 1 = 7(x + 4)$
  (I) $y - 0 = 7(x - 4)$

6. $(^-8, 2)$, $m = ^-5$
  (S) $y - 2 = ^-5(x + 8)$
  (J) $x - 2 = ^-5(y + 8)$

7. $(4, 6)$, $m = ^-10$
  (W) $x - 4 = ^-10(y - 6)$
  (S) $y - 6 = ^-10(x - 4)$

8. $(9, ^-1)$, $m = 0$
  (I) $y + 1 = 0(x - 9)$
  (O) $y - 0 = 1(x + 9)$

9. $(^-3, ^-7)$, $m = 9$
  (Y) $x + 7 = 9(y + 3)$
  (S) $y + 7 = 9(x + 3)$

10. $(9, 3)$, $m = ^-1$
  (S) $y - 3 = ^-1(x - 9)$
  (T) $y + 9 = ^-1(x + 3)$

11. $(6, ^-7)$, $m = ^-4$
  (G) $x - 7 = ^-4(y + 6)$
  (I) $y + 7 = ^-4(x - 6)$

12. $(11, ^-2)$, $m = 1$
  (P) $y + 2 = x - 11$
  (K) $y - 2 = x + 11$

13. $(1, ^-5)$, $m = 5$
  (L) $y - 5 = ^-5(x + 1)$
  (P) $y + 5 = 5(x - 1)$

14. $(1, ^-1)$, $m = 2$
  (I) $y + 1 = 2(x - 1)$
  (R) $y - 1 = 2(x + 1)$

___ ___ ___   ___ ___ ___ ___ ___ ___ ___ ___ ___ ___
1   2   3   4   5   6   7   8   9   10   11   12   13   14

Calculating Absolute Values and Inequalities

Every algebra student will greatly benefit from the activities involving calculating absolute values and inequalities in this section. Allow students ample opportunity to work with manipulatives and time to complete several examples with your guidance. Be sure students gain a conceptual understanding of the concepts to the right before proceeding through the independent student activity pages (pages 38–47).

Present everyday situations to students in which they may use their new skills. For example, students can use their knowledge of calculating absolute values and inequalities when working with records in sports, popular trends, or figures of profits over expenses. Help students observe the world in which they live and identify their own connections involving calculating absolute values and inequalities.

CONCEPTS

The ideas and activities presented in this section will help students explore the following concepts:

- absolute value equations
- absolute value graphs
- inequalities with one variable
- compound inequalities
- inequalities with absolute value
- inequalities with two variables
- inequality graphs

GETTING STARTED

Ask students to explain the meaning of the words *and* and *or*. How do they use them every day? In what ways are these meanings related and in what ways are they different? Go through several examples with students of the everyday use of these two words in compound English sentences. Ask students where these words are found in math and give them several examples using number sentences. (They are found in compound inequalities. $4 < x < 10 \rightarrow$ and; $^-1 < x < 0 \rightarrow$ and; $x < ^-2$ or $x > 5 \rightarrow$ or; $x < ^-7$ or $x > ^-1 \rightarrow$ or)

QUICK MOTIVATORS

- Ask students to come up with the everyday meaning of *inequalities*. Have them give some real life examples of comparisons involving the words *equal, not equal, greater than*, and *less than*.

- Write the following inequalities on the board:

$2 < 7$ $^-2 > ^-4$ $5 > ^-3$ $^-3 < 1$

	x 2	x $^-3$
	$4 < 14$	$^-6 > ^-21$
	$^-4 > ^-8$	$6 < 12$
	$10 > ^-6$	$^-15 < 9$
	$^-6 < 2$	$9 > ^-3$

Have students multiply both sides of each inequality by 2 and then by $^-3$. Be sure to tell them to use the correct inequality symbols. Ask students to calculate the results and explain in detail their conclusions.

(When multiplying by a positive number, the inequality symbol did not change. You must flip the inequality symbol when multiplying by a negative number.)

- Ask students to explain the meaning of these words: *at most, at least, not greater than, not less than*, and *between*. They may use sentences to represent their meanings. Be sure to have students relate these to math and give examples.

FUN WITH MATH

Put the problems below on the board to get students on track and into algebra.

- A musical CD and a tape cassette sell together for $25. If the CD alone costs more than two cassettes but less than three cassettes, what could the cost of the CD be? (between $16.67 and $18.75)

- Jory Jones has five brothers and sisters: Sally, Joe, Tony, Suzie, and Jake. Jory is the youngest. Joe is between Tony and Jake. Tony is more years older than Jory than Sally is. Suzie is between Jory and Sally. Suzie is not next to the youngest. Joe is between Sally and Suzie. Starting with Jory being the youngest, what is the order of the rest of the siblings? (Jory, Jake, Suzie, Joe, Sally, Tony)

DEMONSTRATING MATH IDEAS

- Ask students to work with a partner. Tell them that they want to bike 20 miles in 30 minutes, at the most. Have them write an inequality to show how fast they must bike. Then have them solve it. ($^{20}/_b \leq \frac{1}{2}$, $b \geq 40$)

- Tell students to draw a rectangle with an area of at least 50 square inches. The length of the rectangle should be 15 inches. Ask your students to write and solve the inequality showing the width of the rectangle. ($15w \geq 60$; $w \geq 4$)

- Ask students to write an absolute value inequality for each graph below.

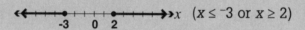

$(^-2 < x < 4)$ $(x \leq ^-3 \text{ or } x \geq 2)$

Chapter Group Project

Ask students to write down five of their interests or hobbies. Have them pick a field of study that most relates to these. Ask students to imagine that they are going to study this field at the nearby university. Have them investigate possible careers in their fields of interest at the local library. How do these careers relate to their interests and hobbies? Ask them to explain their reasoning and investigation.

Some possible questions to ask students are these:

- Which career would offer the most amount of money?
- Which careers might offer a greater amount of money having more than a bachelor's degree?
- Which careers require a degree for which the years studied are greater than the number of years required for a bachelor's degree?
- Which career would you choose? Write an inequality expressing the time needed to study and train for your particular career of choice.

EXPLORING EXTENSIONS

- Ask students to graph $y = ^-3x + 2$. Have them use the graph to solve the inequality $^-3x + 2 > 0$. Be sure students explain their reasoning. ($x < ^2/_3$)

- Ask students to write a compound inequality describing the possible lenghts of the side of each triangle below marked with an x. Students should use the fact that the sum of the lengths of any two sides of the triangle is greater than the length of the third side.

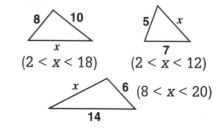

(2 < x < 18)   (2 < x < 12)

(8 < x < 20)

*S*choolin' *S*kunk

What do you think a skunk has to do before it goes to school?

To find out, complete each problem table by substituting each x value into the equation and solving for y. Find the code letters that match the y values and write the letters in the spaces provided to spell out each of the five words in the answer.

A	C	G	H	I	K	N	O	P	S	T	U
8	12	⁻4	2	⁻2	⁻8	4	⁻1	0	⁻9	⁻6	⁻3

1. $y = {}^-3|x - 1| + 3$

x	0	⁻1	⁻2
y			

1st word in the answer: _____

2. $y = {}^-|x - 5| + 5$

x	11	
y		

2nd word in the answer: _____

3. $y = |x + 2| - 10$

x	6	2	⁻3
y			

3rd word in the answer: _____

4. $y = {}^-2|x - 4| + 8$

x	12.5	⁻3	⁻1	2	⁻4	9	6	⁻2
y								

4th word in the answer: _____

5. $y = 4|x - 1| - 4$

x	5	⁻2	2
y			

5th word in the answer: _____

Answer: _____

FS122010 Algebra Made Simple • © Carson-Dellosa

Towering Tallness

The tallest man in the world that ever lived is known to have been 8 feet 11 ¹⁄₁₀ inches tall. He was born on February 22, 1918, in Alton, Illinois. He weighed 491 pounds. What is the name of this famous man?

To find out, solve for x. Circle the letter that is next to the solution for each equation. Read the circled letters downward to reveal the two-word answer.

1. $|x + 2| = 4$ (R) $x = 2, \ ^-6$ (S) $x = \ ^-2, \ ^-6$

2. $|x + 3| = 11$ (A) $x = \ ^-14, \ ^-8$ (O) $x = \ ^-14, 8$

3. $|x - 9| = 14$ (M) $x = 5, 23$ (B) $x = 23, \ ^-5$

4. $4 + |x - 2| = 7$ (E) $x = 5, \ ^-1$ (U) $x = \ ^-5, 1$

5. $^-4 + |x + 1| = 10$ (R) $x = 13, \ ^-15$ (L) $x = \ ^-13, \ ^-15$

6. $^-|x - 9| = \ ^-12$ (J) $x = 3, \ ^-21$ (T) $x = \ ^-3, 21$

7. $^-12 + |x - 1| = 3$ (W) $x = \ ^-14, 16$ (A) $x = 14, \ ^-16$

8. $4 - |x + 6| = 3$ (C) $x = 7, 5$ (A) $x = \ ^-7, \ ^-5$

9. $|x + 3| - 8 = 10$ (D) $x = 15, \ ^-21$ (K) $x = \ ^-15, 21$

10. $|^-2x + 4| = 8$ (S) $x = 2, 6$ (L) $x = \ ^-2, 6$

11. $|3x - 9| - 3 = 12$ (O) $x = 8, \ ^-2$ (U) $x = \ ^-8, 2$

12. $4 - |x - 6| = \ ^-2$ (N) $x = 0, \ ^-12$ (W) $x = 0, 12$

Answer: _____

Best Barber

Why did the barber win the race?

To find out, calculate the vertex of each absolute value equation below. Write each answer in the blank next to its problem number. Shade in the boxes that contain your solutions. Read across the remaining unshaded boxes to spell out the five-word answer to the race riddle.

1. $y = |x - 3| + 6$ V = _____

2. $y = {}^-3|x + 4| - 5$ V = _____

3. $y = |x - 1|$ V = _____

4. $y = {}^-6|x + 9| - 9$ V = _____

5. $y = {}^-5|x - 2| + 3$ V = _____

6. $y = {}^-6|x| + 4$ V = _____

7. $y = |x + 1| - 1$ V = _____

8. $y = |x|$ V = _____

9. $y = {}^-8|x + 8|$ V = _____

10. $y = {}^-7|x| + 9$ V = _____

H	T	E	O	K
(⁻3, 6)	(⁻9, ⁻9)	(9, 9)	(0, 0)	(0, 1)
N	**E**	**Y**	**R**	**W**
(0, 10)	(8, 3)	(3, 6)	(0, 9)	(5, 4)
A	**C**	**S**	**H**	**J**
(⁻3, 5)	(2, 3)	(1, 1)	(⁻4, 0)	(⁻4, ⁻5)
O	**F**	**R**	**K**	**T**
(7, 6)	(0, 4)	(⁻1, 1)	(⁻8, 0)	(9, ⁻9)
H	**C**	**O**	**U**	**T**
(1, 0)	(⁻2, ⁻3)	(⁻1, ⁻1)	(8, 1)	(4, 5)

Answer: _____

Popular Hot-Spot

According to the World Tourism Organization, this country received over 60,584,000 foreign tourists in 1995. What country is known to have the most tourism in the world?

To find out, calculate the vertex of the graph for each equation. Match each equation to its corresponding graph. Write the letter of the matching graph in front of the problem number to spell out the answer.

_____ **1.** $y = |x + 3| - 2$ V = _____

_____ **2.** $y = {}^-|x - 6| + 5$ V = _____

_____ **3.** $y = 3|x + 2| + 1$ V = _____

_____ **4.** $y = {}^-10|x - 5| + 4$ V = _____

_____ **5.** $y = |x + 1| - 1$ V = _____

_____ **6.** $y = {}^-4|x - 4| + 4$ V = _____

N.

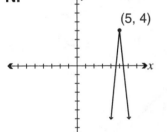

R.

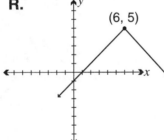

S.

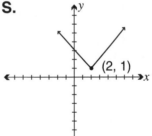

E.

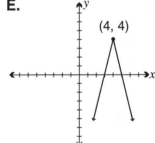

C.

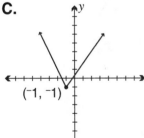

I.

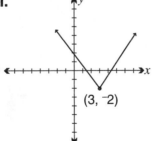

A.

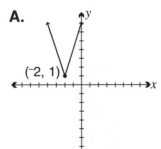

F.

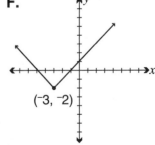

Answer: _____

Home Run-a-Rama

Twelve players have achieved a world record made in baseball history. They hold the record for the most home runs ever hit in a single game. How many home runs is this?

To find out, draw the V-graph of each absolute value equation on a separate sheet of graph paper. Count the number of graphs that open up. Your total will equal the "home run" answer.

1. $y = {}^-2|x - 2|$

2. $y = |x - 1| + 3$

3. $y = {}^-|x + 4| - 1$

4. $y = {}^-|x| + 5$

5. $y = 3|x - 2| + 4$

6. $y = {}^-7|x + 3|$

7. $y = 6|x|$

8. $y = {}^-\frac{1}{2}|x - 4| - 2$

9. $y = |x - 5| + 1$

10. $y = {}^-4|x - 3| - 5$

Answer: _____

FS122010 Algebra Made Simple ▪ © Carson-Dello

Hole-in-One

What do you get when you cross a card with a game of golf?

To find out, solve each equation for x. To spell out the answer, write the letter of the corresponding problem above the given answer.

T. $x + 4 < 14$

E. $26 - x > 34$

A. $x - 12 \geq 7$

H. $65 - x \leq 63$

I. $^-x - 18 < 4$

N. $x - 12 > 35$

O. $8 - x < 10$

H. $^-6x < 18$

A. $^-5 + x \geq 6$

E. $3x - 3 \geq 15$

E. $^-x - 13 > 1$

C. $^-4x - 8 < 16$

L. $x - 12 \leq 13$

N. $15 + 17x \leq {}^-19$

$\overline{}$ $\overline{}$ $\overline{}$ $\overline{}$ $\overline{}$ $\overline{}$ $\overline{}$
$x \geq 11$ $x > 47$ $x \geq 19$ $x > {}^-6$ $x < {}^-8$ $x > {}^-22$ $x \leq {}^-2$

$\overline{}$ $\overline{}$ $\overline{}$ $\overline{}$ $\overline{}$ $\overline{}$ $\overline{}$ **!**
$x < 10$ $x \geq 2$ $x \geq 6$ $x > {}^-3$ $x > {}^-2$ $x \leq 25$ $x < {}^-14$

Motoring Through Math

Which state builds more cars and trucks than any other state in the United States? (Hint: This state is the only state touched by four of the five Great Lakes and the only state divided into two parts.)

To find out, solve the compound inequalities for x below. Match each compound inequality in Column A to its graph in Column B. Read down the column of written letters to discover the answer.

Column A

_____ **1.** $^-6 \geq x - 4 > 4$

_____ **2.** $^-4 \leq 3 - x \leq 2$

_____ **3.** $22 > ^-4x - 18 > ^-58$

_____ **4.** $6 - 2x > 20$ or $8 - x \leq 0$

_____ **5.** $^-12 \leq 2x - 6 < 4$

_____ **6.** $2 > 8x - 14 > 26$

_____ **7.** $^-3x \leq ^-27$ or $2x - 8 \leq 6$

_____ **8.** $^-2x > 6$ or $x - 7 \geq ^-2$

Column B

H.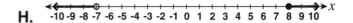

G.

N.

M.

I.

A.

C.

I.

O.

B.

R.

Answer: _____

FS122010 Algebra Made Simple ▪ © Carson-Dellos

Computer Caught

Which way did the rascal go when it stole a computer?

To find out, solve each equation. Identify the graph that matches each solution. Next to each graph, write the letter representing the given equation. Read the letters next to the graphs from left to right to reveal the two-word answer.

A. $|x - 2| > 1$

A. $|^-3 + 2x| \leq 9$

W. $|2x + 5| \leq 3$

D. $|x + 4| < 7$

T. $|2x + 3| < 9$

A. $|5 - 4x| \leq 3$

Y. $|4x - 8| \geq 20$

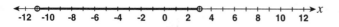

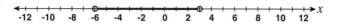

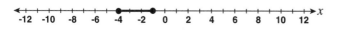

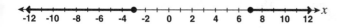

Answer: _____

Golf Master

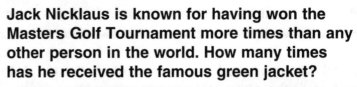

Jack Nicklaus is known for having won the Masters Golf Tournament more times than any other person in the world. How many times has he received the famous green jacket?

To find out, write yes if the ordered pair is a solution; write no if it is not for each inequality. Count the number of yes answers. Your total will equal the amount of Masters wins for Mr. Nicklaus.

_____ **1.** $^-x - y < 5$, (4, 1)

_____ **2.** $5x - 3y \geq 10$, ($^-9$, 7)

_____ **3.** $4x - 3y < 2$, ($^-2$, 4)

_____ **4.** $y > 5x + 7$, ($^-2$, $^-4$)

_____ **5.** $^-11x - y \geq 4$, ($^-3$, 15)

_____ **6.** $9x + 6y < 14$, ($^-1$, 3)

_____ **7.** $y \geq {}^-3x + 6$, ($^-10$, $^-9$)

_____ **8.** $31x - 22y < {}^-12$, (1, 2)

_____ **9.** $y \leq {}^-2x - 23$, (5, $^-2$)

_____ **10.** $15x + 20y \geq 0$, (3, $^-2$)

Answer: _____

Sellin' Single

In March 1985, "We Are the World," sung by USA for Africa, was the fastest selling single ever made in the world. It sold over 800,000 copies in a matter of days. How many days was this?

To find out, graph each inequality on a separate sheet of paper. Count the number of graphs you shaded <u>above</u> each line (rather than below each line). Your total will equal the unbelievable number of days.

1. $6x - 6y \geq 12$

2. $y \leq {}^-5x - 1$

3. $2x - y \leq 4$

4. $y \leq 3$

5. $14x - 7y \leq {}^-28$

6. $y \geq {}^-2$

7. ${}^-6x + 2y \leq {}^-10$

8. $9x + 3y \leq {}^-12$

9. ${}^-x - y \geq 3$

10. $y \leq {}^-2x + 4$

Answer: _____

Solving and Graphing Linear Systems

Every algebra student will greatly benefit from the activities involving solving and graphing linear systems in this section. Allow students ample opportunity to work with manipulatives and time to complete several examples with your guidance. Be sure students gain a conceptual understanding of the concepts below before proceeding through the independent student activity pages (pages 50–55).

Present everyday situations to students in which they may use their new skills. For example, students can use their knowledge of solving and graphing linear systems when modeling multiple investments, comparing costs, and studying compositions of different mixtures and compounds. Help students observe the world in which they live and identify their own connections involving solving and graphing linear systems.

CONCEPTS

The ideas and activities presented in this section will help students explore the following concepts:

- identifying solutions to linear systems
- graphing linear systems
- using substitution in linear systems
- using linear combinations in linear systems
- special linear systems
- linear inequality systems

GETTING STARTED

To introduce systems of linear equations, ask students to tell you at how many points two straight lines drawn in the same plane will intersect. (exactly 1 point) Have them explain in detail the relationship of these lines. Are they parallel, intersecting, or coincidental? What is the meaning of each of these three names of lines? Give several examples of the methods used to conclude such solutions to linear systems, which students will study throughout this section.

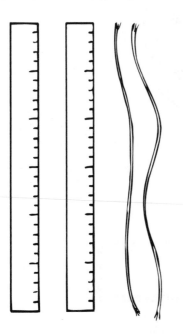

QUICK MOTIVATORS

- Ask students to compare the differences between using two rulers to find points of intersection and using two pieces of string. Have them write their conclusions in detailed explanations. They should find that two rulers yield exactly one point of intersection, and two pieces of string yield infinitely many points of intersection. Ask them to explain how and why this is possible.

- Ask students to give several ordered pairs that are solutions to the equation, $y = 3x - 4$. Have them graph the solutions and conclude what is true about them. Ask students to give several ordered pairs that are solutions to the equation $y = x + 2$. What is true about these solutions when graphed? Ask students to find the ordered pair that is a solution for both of these equations. (3, 5) What does this mean? (The point is the intersection of the two lines.)

FS122010 Algebra Made Simple ▪ © Carson-Dellosa

FUN WITH MATH

Put the problems below on the board to get students on track and into algebra.

- Richie and Sara finished their group project for math class in 18 minutes, working together. If they had to do the project alone, Sara would have had to work 15 minutes longer than Richie to complete her project on time. How long would it have taken Sara to do the entire project herself? (45 minutes)

- Find the values of x, y, and z that make the statements below all true. ($x = 2$, $y = {}^-1$, $z = 4$)

$$y + z = 3 \qquad {}^-2x - y + z = 1 \qquad x - 3y - 2z = {}^-3$$

DEMONSTRATING MATH IDEAS

Ask students to explain what it means to solve a linear system. Have them use the graph-and-check method to solve the system below. (2, 4)

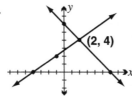

$$x + y = 6 \qquad {}^-2x + 3y = 8$$

Ask students to sketch the graphs of the systems of linear inequalities below. Have them describe each solution.

$x < 0$
$y > 0$
(values of x and y in Quadrant 2)

$x \geq 0$
$y \leq 0$
${}^-x + y > 4$
(x and y values only in Quadrant 1)

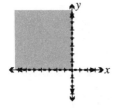

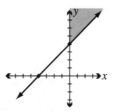

EXPLORING EXTENSIONS

- Ask students to find the dimensions of a rectangle if the area is x and the perimeter is $2x + 2$. The length of the shorter side is $y + 5$, and the length of the longest side is 15. (15 x 1)

- Ask students to complete each of the systems below with the constants that will yield each given solution.

$${}^-3x - 5y = {}^-35$$
$$\tfrac{1}{5}x + 6y = 25$$
solution: (5, 4)

$$9x - 7y = {}^-39$$
$${}^-x + 2y = 8$$
solution: ($^-2$, 3)

Chapter Group Project

Ask students to imagine that they are entering into a bicycle race across the country. Each of them has one friend with them that they are competing against. Suppose that student #1's speed is 50 mph, and student #2 is 275 feet ahead in the race, racing at 40 mph.

Ask each student to write a system of equations representing the situation. What must they do before they can do this? Have them explain what must be converted before they set up this system and why. If their speed does remain constant, when would student #1 catch up with student #2? Ask them to explain this using their solutions and through graphing.

When students finish this part of the project, have them come up with their own situation which can be solved using linear systems. Once they have created this and found its solution, have them switch with their partner, solving one another's situations and systems. Ask them to explain in detail the process they used and how the solution they came up with relates directly to its situation.

Name

Radio Raves

Why did the car radio have to go see a mechanic?

To find out, circle the letter in each problem that represents the solution to the linear system. Then write the corresponding letter above its problem number at the bottom of the page.

1. $x + y = 9$
$-2x + y = -3$

(H) (4, -2)
(F) (4, 5)

6. $2x + y = -4$
$5x + 3y = -6$

(Y) (6, 5)
(U) (-6, 8)

2. $-x + y = 7$
$x + y = 9$

(O) (1, 8)
(U) (9, 2)

7. $x + y = 8$
$-4x + y = -7$

(N) (3, 5)
(O) (-2, 7)

3. $x + y = 27$
$3x - y = 41$

(T) (-7, 10)
(R) (17, 10)

8. $4x + 3y = 24$
$5x - 8y = -17$

(G) (-4, -3)
(E) (3, 4)

4. $x + y = 6$
$y = 3$

(A) (3, 3)
(I) (-3, 3)

9. $3x - 2y = 11$
$x - \frac{1}{2}y = 4$

(U) (5, 2)
(K) (-5, 3)

5. $x + 2y = 1$
$2x + y = 5$

(T) (3, -1)
(S) (4, 2)

10. $x + 4y = 8$
$2x - 5y = 29$

(L) (6, -5)
(P) (12, -1)

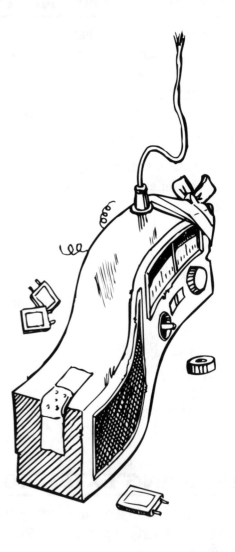

___ ___ ___   ___   ___ ___ ___ ___   - ___   ___ ___!
 1   2   3   4   5   6   7   8   9   10

Scary Skidding

Craig Breedlove, driving the jet-powered Spirit of America, lost control of the car at Bonneville Salt Flats, Utah, on October 15, 1964. He holds the record for the longest skid marks ever made in the world. How long were these amazing marks?

To find out, solve each linear system below by graphing. To reveal the record answer at the bottom of the page, write the letter of each problem above its solution.

S. $^-x + y = ^-1$
  $x + y = 3$

I. $4x + 3y = 24$
  $3x - 11y = 18$

M. $^-2x + y = ^-1$
  $3x + y = 4$

I. $2x + y = ^-4$
  $5x + 3y = ^-6$

L. $y = 10$
  $y = 3x + 1$

S. $2x + y = 9$
  $^-4x + y = ^-3$

X. $2x + 3y = 0$
  $3x - 2y = ^-13$

E. $x = ^-3$
  $^-2x + y = 1$

$\overline{}$ $\overline{}$ $\overline{}$ $\quad$ $\overline{}$ $\overline{}$ $\overline{}$ $\overline{}$ $\overline{}$
(2, 5) (⁻6, 8) (⁻3, 2)   (1, 1) (6, 0) (3, 10) (⁻3, ⁻5) (2, 1)

In the Lead

This famous actor starred in movies from 1927 to 1976. He appeared in 153 movies and played the lead in all but 11 of them. Who was this famous man, still holding the record for the most leading roles in movies?

To find out, solve each linear system below using the substitution method. Find your solution in the list of answers provided and write the letters by the corresponding problem numbers to spell out the two-word answer.

_____ **1.** $y = x$
$3x - y = {}^-4$

_____ **2.** $3x - 5y = {}^-9$
$4x + y = {}^-12$

_____ **3.** $3x - y = 12$
$4x - 5y = 16$

_____ **4.** $4x + 3y = 3$
$x + 2y = 2$

_____ **5.** $y = 2x - 6$
$x = y + 4$

_____ **6.** $x - y = {}^-1$
${}^-2x + 3y = 5$

_____ **7.** $y = 5x + 4$
$y = {}^-2x - 3$

_____ **8.** $5x + 4y = 0$
$x - y = 9$

_____ **9.** $2x - y = {}^-1$
$x - 2y = {}^-11$

N (4, ⁻5)

E (3, 7)

H (4, 0)

J (⁻2, ⁻2)

Y (⁻1, ⁻1)

N (0, 1)

O (⁻3, 0)

W (2, ⁻2)

A (2, 3)

Answer: _____

FS122010 Algebra Made Simple ▪ © Carson-Dellosa

Golden Champion

Mark Spitz, a United States Olympic swimmer, holds the record for the most gold medals ever won in one Olympics. He received these medals at the Olympic Games in Munich in 1972, in the freestyle, butterfly, and relay events. How many gold medals did he win?

To find out, solve each linear system using the linear combination method. Shade in the boxes that contain your solutions. Read across the unshaded boxes to identify the answer.

1. $x - 2y = 2$
   $2x + 2y = 1$

2. $x + 3y = 1$
   $^-x + y = 7$

3. $^-2x + 3y = 2$
   $2x + 7y = 18$

4. $3x + 7y = 3$
   $x - 7y = 1$

5. $5x - 4y = 1$
   $7x + 4y = 11$

6. $x + 3y = 2$
   $2x + 4y = ^-2$

7. $^-3x + 5y = 9$
   $^-4x - y = 12$

8. $x - y = ^-1$
   $2x - 3y = ^-5$

9. $3x - y = 12$
   $4x - 5y = 16$

S	R	E	P	O	G
(0, 7)	(1, 0)	(5, 2)	(2, 3)	(⁻5, 2)	(1, 1)
V	**I**	**M**	**E**	**U**	**N**
(⁻2, ⁻3)	(1, ⁻½)	(4, 0)	(⁻2, 2)	(⁻7, 3)	(⁻1, 1)
G	**C**	**O**	**L**	**H**	**D**
(⁻½, 1)	(⁻3, 0)	(7, ⁻3)	(3, 0)	(2, 2)	(⁻4, 0)

Answer: _____

Cross Combination

What would you get if you crossed an insect with a rabbit?

To find out, graph each linear system on a separate piece of paper. From the pair of answers provided, select the one that describes the graph and circle the corresponding letter. Read down the circled letters to identify the two-word answer.

1. $2x - y = 6$
$x - \frac{1}{2}y = 3$
    (B) Has many solutions   (I) Has no solution

2. $^-3x + 5y = 12$
$3x - 5y = 15$
    (N) Has many solutions   (U) Has no solution

3. $8x + 2y = 13$
$4x + y = 11$
    (D) Has many solutions   (G) Has no solution

4. $^-6x + 2y = 4$
$^-3x + y = 2$
    (S) Has many solutions   (E) Has no solution

5. $x + y = 16$
$2x + 2y = 2$
    (R) Has many solutions   (B) Has no solution

6. $\frac{5}{2}x + y = 4$
$5x + 2y = 8$
    (U) Has many solutions   (T) Has no solution

7. $3x + 4y = 7$
$\frac{3}{2}x + 2y = 11$
    (F) Has many solutions   (N) Has no solution

8. $x + 5y = 4$
$3x + 15y = ^-1$
    (M) Has many solutions   (N) Has no solution

9. $x - 5y = 10$
$2x - 10y = 20$
    (Y) Has many solutions   (A) Has no solution

Answer: _____

Album Astonishment

What is the best-selling album of all time, with global sales of 47 million and domestic sales of over 25 million? (After you find this answer, do you know which singer made this album?)

To find the answer, graph each system of linear inequalities. In front of each problem number, write the letter representing the quadrant(s) where the solution can be found. Read down the column of letters to identify the answer.

Column A

_____ **1.** $y \geq -1$

$x \geq -2$

_____ **2.** $3x - 5y \geq -25$

$y \geq 0, x \leq 0$

_____ **3.** $y \geq x$

$y \leq x + 3$

_____ **4.** $y \leq x$

$2x - y \geq 3$

_____ **5.** $y \geq -x$

$y \geq x$

_____ **6.** $x \geq 0, y \geq 0$

$x + 2y \leq 6$

_____ **7.** $x \geq 5$

$y \leq 4$

_____ **8.** $y + x \leq 4$

$y - x \geq 4$

Column B

L. Quadrants I and II

H. Quadrant II

R. Quadrants I, II, and III

I. Quadrants I, III, and IV

R. Quadrants II and III

T. Quadrants I, II, III, and IV

E. Quadrants I and IV

L. Quadrant I

Answer: _____

Working With Exponents

Every algebra student will greatly benefit from the activities involving working with exponents in this section. Allow students ample opportunity to work with manipulatives and time to complete several examples with your guidance. Be sure students gain a conceptual understanding of the concepts below before proceeding through the independent student activity pages (pages 58–61).

Present everyday situations to students in which they may use their new skills. For example, students can use their knowledge of working with exponents to find exponential change and models of real-life settings and to write very small numbers or extremely large numbers. Help students observe the world in which they live and identify their own connections involving working with exponents.

CONCEPTS

The ideas and activities presented in this section will help students explore the following concepts:

- multiplying exponents
- dividing exponents
- negative and zero exponents
- scientific notation

GETTING STARTED

Tell students that the height of a stack of used computer paper doubles every day after the first. Ask them to use powers of 2 to tell you the height of the stack of paper for an entire week of school (5 days) if the stack was 5 inches high on Monday. [$(5 \cdot 2^0) \cdot (5 \cdot 2^1) \cdot (5 \cdot 2^2) \cdot (5 \cdot 2^3) \cdot (5 \cdot 2^4)$] Ask them to explain their steps and reasoning in detail. Then ask them to calculate how many school days it will take the stack to get over 8 feet high. (6 days) Have them explain the use of exponents in a problem such as this and why this is the appropriate and fastest way to solve the problem.

QUICK MOTIVATORS

- Ask students to multiply a certain number by itself four times so that the sum of the digits in its product is equal to the actual number. Have them tell you the number and explain what other numbers (if any) would also work. (possible answers: 7, 22, 28)

- Ask students to come up with the number x that makes the following statement true: *A number multiplied by itself six times divided by the number multiplied by itself three times is the number multiplied by itself three times.* Is there more than one number for which this is true? Ask students to explain to you, in general, the set of numbers for which this statement will always be true. (The set of real numbers will always make the statement, $\frac{6x}{3x} = 3x$, true.)

FUN WITH MATH

Put the problems below on the board to get students on track and into algebra.

- What is the largest number that can be used as the product of positive integers whose sum is 50? (625; 25 + 25 = 50; 25 • 25 = 625)

- Find the difference between the smallest perfect square larger than 1,000 and the largest perfect square smaller than 1,000. (1024 − 961 = 63)

- Find all x and y values, less than 100 and greater than 0, that make the statement below true.

   $x^2 − y^2 = 48$. (Hint: There are three pairs that will work.) (8, 4), (7, 1), (13, 11)

DEMONSTRATING MATH IDEAS

Ask students to fill in the table of values to the right and answer the questions below.

x	1	2	3
$3x$	? (3)	? (6)	? (9)
3^x	? (3)	? (9)	? (27)

Sketch the graphs of $y = 3x$ and $y = 3^x$ on the same coordinate plane.

Which job would you choose if job A was going to pay you $3x$ dollars for x hours of work and job B was to pay you 3^x dollars for x hours of work? Explain in detail your reasoning for your choice. (3^x for $x > 1$, it pays more)

After an 8-hour day, if your boss asked you to work 3 more hours, how much more money would you make if your hourly pay was 2^x dollars? ($2^{11} − 2^8 = \$1792$)

EXPLORING EXTENSIONS

Ask students to simplify the following expressions:

$x^b • x^b$ (Answer: x^{2b})

$(5^{4x + 5}) • (5^{2x + 3})$ (Answer: $5^{6x + 8}$)

$(x^{b + 4}) ÷ (x^{b − 4})$ (Answer: x^8)

$(x^a) ÷ (x^{a + 2})$ (Answer: x^2)

Ask students to solve the problem below.

The fastest speed of a motorcycle is 1.93×10^4 feet per minute. What is the speed in feet per second and in miles per hour?

($\approx 3.22 \times 10^2$ ft/sec; $\approx 2.19 \times 10^2$ mi/hr)

Chapter Group Project

Divide students into pairs. Each student in the class needs to draw a square, rectangle, triangle, and rectangular solid on a piece of graph paper. Ask students to label one side of the square, the long and shorter side of the rectangle, the base and height of the triangle, and the three edges of the rectangular solid—all of these with monomials. Then have them calculate the area of the square, rectangle, and triangle, and the volume of the rectangular solid.

Once they have completed this task, ask them to switch with their partner to double check each other's work and calculations. Ask each pair to then switch papers with another pair to find the area of each square, rectangle, and triangle, and the volume of each rectangular solid. Be sure each pair agrees on its answers before checking them with other pairs. The final part of this project are the written explanations of how each pair worked its calculations, along with detailed information of why it chose the steps or methods it did.

Balloon Baffled

The largest latex balloon to ever appear in the Macy's Thanksgiving Day parade in New York City was 61 feet long and 35 feet wide. It held 18,907 cubic feet of helium and air. Who did this balloon depict?

To find out, simplify each expression. Write the problem number in front of the corresponding answer listed in the table. To spell out the answer at the bottom of the page, refer to the table and write the code letter that corresponds to the problem number given.

1. $(3x)(x^4)$

2. $(4x^2)(8x^3)$

3. $(x^5)^3$

4. $(3x)(2x^2)(5x^3)$

5. $(^-3x^2)(^-7x)(^-2x^4)$

6. $(^-x^2y)(^-xy^2)(^-xy^4)$

7. $(^-12x)(3x^2y)(^-2y)$

8. $(^-x^2)^3(4x^2)^3$

9. $(^-3xy^3)(x^2y)^4$

10. $(xy)^2(x^3)^4$

11. $(2x^4y)^3$

Code Letter	Problem #	Answer
A		$30x^6$
C		$72x^3y^2$
D		$x^{14}y^2$
E		$32x^5$
F		$^-x^4y^7$
G		$3x^5$
H		$^-64x^{12}$
I		x^{15}
L		$8x^{12}y^3$
R		$^-42x^7$
T		$^-3x^9y^7$

$\overline{}\ \overline{}\ \overline{}\ \overline{}\ \overline{}\ \overline{}\ \overline{}\ \overline{}\qquad \overline{}\ \overline{}\ \overline{}\qquad \overline{}\ \overline{}\ \overline{}$

1   4   5   6   3   2   11   10   9   8   2   7   4   9

Incredible Irony

Believe it or not, the people of Washington, D.C., did not always have the right to vote for the position of President of the United States. How many Presidents had the United States had before these people were allowed to vote?

To find out, simplify each term. Match your answers to those given. Write the letter corresponding to the solution above each problem number at the bottom of the page to spell out the answer.

_____ 1. $\dfrac{x^2y}{xy}$

R. $\dfrac{1}{2x}$

_____ 2. $\dfrac{-2x^2y}{18xy}$

S. $\dfrac{-4x}{3y^3}$

_____ 3. $\dfrac{10x^2y}{10x^2y}$

T. x

_____ 4. $\dfrac{13xy}{26x^2y}$

Y. $\dfrac{-3}{xy}$

_____ 5. $\dfrac{(9y)^3}{9y}$

X. $9x^6$

_____ 6. $\dfrac{-18xy^2}{6x^2y^3}$

H. $\dfrac{-x}{9}$

_____ 7. $\dfrac{-12x^2y}{9xy^4}$

I. $-2y^3$

_____ 8. $\dfrac{(-3xy)(6x^2y^4)}{9x^3y^2}$

T. $81y^2$

_____ 9. $\dfrac{(3x^2)^3(2xy)}{6xy}$

I. 1

‾‾‾‾ ‾‾‾‾ ‾‾‾‾ ‾‾‾‾ ‾‾‾‾ ‾‾‾‾   —   ‾‾‾‾ ‾‾‾‾ ‾‾‾‾
  1   2   3   4   5   6   7   8   9

Money no Matter

In 1997, NBC renewed its contract to produce a sitcom for the 1997–1998 season for a cost of $120 million—the most expensive TV series renewal ever recorded. This show also demanded the most money in television history for advertisement—more than $1 million per minute. What is the name of this famous show?

To find out, simplify each problem below using only positive exponents. Find your answers in the list provided and circle the corresponding letters. Unscramble the circled letters to discover the answer.

1. $2x^{-5}$

2. $-3x^0y^{-1}$

3. $2x^{-5}y^3$

4. $\dfrac{(7x)^0}{4x^0}$

5. $\dfrac{8x}{4^0x^{-4}}$

6. $\dfrac{8x^{-3}y^4}{-2xy^{-5}}$

7. $\dfrac{-6x^{-4}y^3}{2x^0y^{-3}}$

8. $\left(\dfrac{6x^2y^3}{-2xy^{-4}}\right)^0$

I $\dfrac{-3y^6}{x^4}$		**N** $\dfrac{2}{x^5}$	
F $\dfrac{2y^3}{x^5}$		**E** $8x^5$	
D $\dfrac{-3}{y}$		**O** xy^4	
G $-4xy$		**E** $\dfrac{1}{4}$	
R $\dfrac{7}{4}$		**B** $-9x^2y^7$	
S 1		**L** $\dfrac{-4y^9}{x^4}$	

Answer: _____

Solo Success

During his lifetime (1956–1977), this man became known as the most successful solo recording artist of all time. He had over 170 hit singles and over 80 top-selling albums. Who was this famous singer?

To find out, change problems 1–6 from scientific notation to decimal form, and change problems 7–12 from decimal form to scientific notation. Match your answers to those given. Write the letter representing the solution in front of each problem number. Read down the columns of letters to reveal the two-word answer to the question.

_____ **1.** 3.1×10^{-4}

_____ **2.** 8.04×10^5

_____ **3.** 4.6×10^{-3}

_____ **4.** 2×10^3

_____ **5.** 5.62×10^7

_____ **6.** 7.03×10^{-6}

_____ **7.** 5,620,000

_____ **8.** 0.0000078

_____ **9.** 0.0401

_____ **10.** 91,450,000

_____ **11.** 0.0000006

_____ **12.** 123,000

S	J	E	O	P	L
56,200,000	4,600	7.8×10^{-6}	200	0.0000073	9.145×10^7
E	**V**	**S**	**G**	**Y**	**R**
0.00031	0.0046	4.01×10^{-2}	9.145×10^5	1.23×10^5	5.62×10^6
I	**L**	**E**	**C**	**N**	**A**
2,000	804,000	6.0×10^{-7}	5,200,000	80,400	0.0000703

Answer: _____

Solving Square Roots and Quadratic Equations

Every algebra student will greatly benefit from the activities involving solving square roots and quadratic equations in this section. Allow students ample opportunity to work with manipulatives and time to complete several examples with your guidance. Be sure students gain a conceptual understanding of the concepts below before proceeding through the independent student activity pages (pages 64–67).

Present everyday situations to students in which they may use their new skills. For example, students can use their knowledge of solving square roots and quadratic equations to model population growth and to study the motion of falling objects. Help students observe the world in which they live and identify their own connections involving solving square roots and quadratic equations.

CONCEPTS

The ideas and activities presented in this section will help students explore the following concepts:

- squares and square roots
- Pythagorean theorem
- solving quadratic equations
- graphing quadratic equations

GETTING STARTED

Ask students to use their calculators to experiment with square roots. Have them use positive and negative numbers. Ask them to explain what happens when they find the square root of a positive number versus the square root of a negative number. After several examples and explanations, ask students to explain, in their own words, the meaning of *square root*.

QUICK MOTIVATORS

- Ask students to describe the graph of a parabola. Have them draw several parabolas on paper. What everyday objects have this same shape? Have them list at least three examples of common objects with a parabola shape.

- Ask students if using a formula to find the area of a rectangle would be easier and quicker than counting the squares. Use this idea to bring in the formula for finding the solutions to a quadratic equation, demonstrating that using the method of completing the square can be used in developing this quick-and-easy formula.

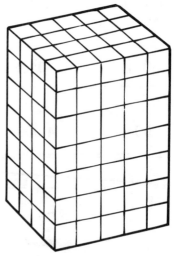

- Ask students how they would solve $x - 9 = 0$. Ask them to tell you the first step in solving $x^2 - 9 = 0$. See if they can give you the number of solutions and the actual solutions to this problem. Have them explain in detail the steps to solve the two problems and the relationship between them.

FUN WITH MATH

Put the problems below on the board to get students on track and into algebra.

- Four squares with areas of 25, 36, 49, and 64 square units are arranged on a grid so that when their vertices coincide, another square is formed. Find the area of the fifth square. (64)

- Factor each of the following expressions as the product of two or more factors:

  $2x^3y - 2xy^3 + x^4 - y^4$

  Answer:

  $(x + y)(x - y)[2xy + (x^2 + y^2)]$

  $25 - 25x - x^2 + x^3$

  Answer: $(1 - x)(25 - x^2)$

- Around the outside of a framed picture, 12 inches long and 5 inches wide, there is a uniform mat border. The area of the entire framed picture is 198 square inches. Find the width of the mat border. (3 inches)

DEMONSTRATING MATH IDEAS

- Ask students to use a calculator to evaluate each expression below. Have them round to two decimal places when necessary.

  $$3\sqrt{14} \qquad 8 - 4\sqrt{2} \qquad [^-6 \pm \sqrt{[6^2 - 7(1)(^-3)]}] \div 3$$
  $$(11.22) \qquad (2.34) \qquad (^+0.52;\ ^-4.52)$$

- Ask students to sketch the quadratic equations below on the same coordinate plane and describe their relationship. Each set should be graphed on its own coordinate plane.

  (1) $y = x^2 \qquad y = x^2 + 2 \qquad y = x^2 - 2$

  (All graphs open up and move up and down on y-axis.)

  (2) $y = ^-x^2 \qquad y = ^-x^2 + 3 \qquad y = ^-x^2 - 3$

  (All graphs open down and move up and down on y-axis.)

EXPLORING EXTENSIONS

- Ask students to simplify each of the positive square roots below. The answers follow each problem.

  $\sqrt{12}$ $(2\sqrt{3})$ $\sqrt{20}$ $(2\sqrt{5})$ $\sqrt{27}$ $(3\sqrt{3})$ $\sqrt{45}$ $(3\sqrt{5})$ $\sqrt{75}$ $(5\sqrt{3})$

- Ask students to sketch all three equations below on the same coordinate plane. Have them give a detailed description of how the three graphs are related.

  $y = x^2 - 2x + 1 \qquad y = x^2 - 4x + 4 \qquad y = x^2 - 6x + 9$

  (All the graphs open up and move along the x-axis increasing by 1 each time.)

Chapter Group Project

Divide students into pairs. Have them do some research on the consumption of energy in the United States for various household products. Some results they may find are as follows:

Household product	% of homes with product	(kilowatts per year) typical energy consumption
refrigerator	67.3	1,591
color TV	99	1,000
computer	15	275
dishwasher	43.1	165
clock	100	40

Ask students to make a graph of the data. Ask them what type of behavior or energy consumption the data represents. Ask them why they think this exists. Have students research in an almanac or statistical abstract to find the average energy use of the United States per year compared to that of other countries. Ask them to make an educated guess as to what this might say for the future use of energy and the future of energy itself.

Drawn-Out Driving

This highway extends 15,000 miles from northwest Alaska to Santiago, Chile, then eastward to Buenos Aires, Argentina, and finally terminates in Brasilia, Brazil. What is the name of this record-holding, longest driveable highway in the world?

To find out, solve each problem. Shade in the boxes that contain your solutions. Read across the unshaded boxes to identify the answer to the question.

1. $\sqrt{25}$

2. $^-\sqrt{64}$

3. $\sqrt{0.16}$

4. $^-\sqrt{121}$

5. $\sqrt{\dfrac{9}{4}}$

6. $^-\sqrt{\dfrac{49}{16}}$

7. $x^2 = 49$

8. $4x^2 = 400$

9. $x^2 + 9 = 25$

10. $10x^2 - 50 = 2200$

11. $7x^2 - 6 = {}^-6$

12. $9x^2 + 12 = 13$

H	P	I	A	U	N
±4	±2	⁻11	⁻0.3	5	±6
A	N	M	Y	E	R
$^-9/2$	±15	12	0	±1	½
J	I	S	C	A	T
±7	⁻16	0.4	$^-5/4$	±20	⁻8
N	H	E	I	W	G
14	±⅑	±⅓	⁻9	³⁄₂	⁻30
H	L	W	A	V	Y
13	±10	±17	±⅘	$^-7/4$	22

Answer: _____

Glass Gallant

On May 18, 1996, Ashrita Furman of Jamaica, New York, made the Guinness Book of World Records when he balanced pint glasses from his chin for 11.89 seconds. How many of these pint glasses did he balance?

To find out, use the Pythagorean theorem to solve for the missing value in each problem. (Round decimals to the nearest hundredth.) Match each set of values in Column A to its matching solution in Column B. Read down the column of written letters to reveal the answer.

Column A	Column B
_____ **1.** $a = 8, c = 17, b = ?$	**S.** 9.54
_____ **2.** $a = 6, b = 2, c = ?$	**E.** 9.80
_____ **3.** $a = 6, b = 8, c = ?$	**F.** 10
_____ **4.** $b = 20, c = 29, a = ?$	**I.** 6.32
_____ **5.** $a = 7, c = 25, b = ?$	**E.** 30
_____ **6.** $a = 3, c = 10, b = ?$	**N.** 40
_____ **7.** $b = 40, c = 50, a = ?$	**Y.** 24
_____ **8.** $a = 1, b = 3, c = ?$	**F.** 15
_____ **9.** $b = 5, c = 11, a = ?$	**V.** 3.16
_____**10.** $a = 9, c = 41, b = ?$	**T.** 21

Answer: _____

Astronaut-ical Math

If astronauts do all of their homework and receive good grades, what do they receive?

To find out, determine the solutions to each quadratic equation. To reveal the answer at the bottom of the page, write the letter of each problem above its solutions.

D. $x^2 + 7x + 12 = 0$

T. $x^2 + 4x - 12 = 0$

R. $2x^2 + 20x + 32 = 0$

S. $3x^2 + 9x - 12 = 0$

O. $x^2 - 7x + 6 = 0$

S. $x^2 - 5x - 24 = 0$

A. $x^2 - 8x + 12 = 0$

L. $x^2 - 2x - 15 = 0$

G. $x^2 + 6x + 8 = 0$

| $x = {}^-2$ | $x = 1$ | $x = {}^-3$ | $x = {}^-3$ | | $x = {}^-3$ | $x = {}^-6$ | $x = 2$ | $x = {}^-8$ | $x = {}^-4$ |
| $x = {}^-4$ | $x = 6$ | $x = 5$ | $x = {}^-4$ | | $x = 8$ | $x = 2$ | $x = 6$ | $x = {}^-2$ | $x = 1$ |

FS122010 Algebra Made Simple ▪ © Carson-Dellosa

Golfing Grandeur

Coby Orr of Littleton, Colorado, is known to be the youngest person to have shot a hole in one in golf. He shot this hole in one on the 103-yard fifth hole at Riverside Golf Course in San Antonio, Texas, in 1975. How old was he?

To find out, draw the graph (parabola) of each quadratic equation on a separate piece of paper. Count the number of parabolas that open up. Your total will equal the answer to this golf record.

1. $y = x^2 + 6x + 8$

2. $y = 2x^2 - 8x + 5$

3. $y = {}^-x^2 - 8x - 15$

4. $y = {}^-x^2$

5. $y = {}^-x^2 - 6x - 8$

6. $y = x^2 - 4x + 5$

7. $y = {}^-x^2 - 4$

8. $y = 2x^2 + 12x + 9$

9. $y = x^2 - 4x + 7$

10. $y = {}^-x^2 - 6x - 7$

Answer: _____

Simplifying Polynomials

Every algebra student will greatly benefit from the activities involving simplifying polynomials in this section. Allow students ample opportunity to work with manipulatives and time to complete several examples with your guidance. Be sure students gain a conceptual understanding of the concepts below before proceeding through the independent student activity pages (pages 70–74).

Present everyday situations to students in which they may use their new skills. For example, students can use their knowledge of simplifying polynomials when studying the performance of something over an interval of time and when modeling a rate times some quantity. Help students observe the world in which they live and identify their own connections involving simplifying polynomials.

CONCEPTS

The ideas and activities presented in this section will help students explore the following concepts:

- adding polynomials
- subtracting polynomials
- multiplying polynomials
- factoring polynomials
- factoring quadratic equations

GETTING STARTED

To develop the idea and understanding of polynomials, try the following activity: Start with the first row of students in your classroom. Ask the first student in the row to come up with a monomial with a degree greater than 2. Have the second student in the same row come up with a monomial term to add to this first monomial to create a binomial. Ask the third student to add yet another term to the binomial to create a trinomial. Have the fourth student identify the degree of the trinomial created by his or her row. Repeat this procedure until all students have had at least one turn coming up with a monomial and one turn identifying the degree of their row's trinomial.

QUICK MOTIVATORS

- Ask students to name some of the operations they have used when solving problems with positive and negative numbers. Ask them to explain how these same operations can be used with polynomials.

- Ask students what the term *4x* is called. (monomial) Is *4x* – 2 a monomial, too? (no) If not, what is this called? (binomial) If you add one more term to *4x* – 2, then what would you have? (trinomial)

- Show students an example of multiplying two binomials using the Distributive Property. Then, using the same binomials, use the FOIL Method to compute the multiplication. Ask students what the differences are in using these two methods and also what the similarities are in using these methods. Which one would they choose to use and why?

Polynomials

FUN WITH MATH

Put the problems below on the board to get students on track and into algebra.

- Imagine you jogged in a 10-km race. You finished 20 minutes behind the winner of the race and ran at an average of 3 km/h less than the winner. What was the winner's average speed throughout the race? (Answer: 15 km/h)

- Find all values of x so that the equation below is true. $(2/x) + (x/2) = (4/x) + (x/4)$ (Answer: $\pm\sqrt{8}$)

- Find the value of x so that the equation below is true. $(1989 - x)^2 = x^2$ (Answer: 994.5)

EXPLORING EXTENSIONS

Ask students to multiply a and b below.

a. $(x + 2)(x - 3)(x + 8)$ b. $(3x + 2)(x + 5)(4x - 3)$

$[a = x^3 + 7x^2 - 14x - 48; \ b = 12x^3 + 59x^2 - 11x - 30]$

Ask students to find the perimeter of the rectangle and square below, given their areas. They can find the length of the sides by factoring the expression.

area = $x^2 - 36$

(P = 4x)

area = $x^2 + 4x + 4$

(P = 4x + 8)

DEMONSTRATING MATH IDEAS

- Ask students to write the meaning of the following prefixes used in algebra: *poly*, *mono*, *bi*, and *tri*. Have students give several examples of these prefixes in words used every day and their meanings. How do these relate to the mathematical meaning?

- Ask students to construct an area model of the polynomial products below.

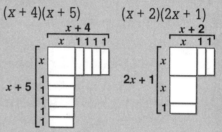

$(x + 4)(x + 5)$ $(x + 2)(2x + 1)$

- Ask students to tell you whether the trinomials below are the square of a binomial. Have them explain their answers.

$4x^2 - 28x + 49$ $2x^2 + 6x + 9$
[yes; $(2x - 7)^2$]   (no; $2x^2$ is not a perfect square)

Chapter Group Project

Divide students into groups of three. Tell students to pretend that they are able to work in the summer and save $3,000. Each will invest his or her money in a savings account at a local bank. To find the value of each year's savings, they can use the expression px^t, where p is the amount invested, x is the sum of 1 and the annual interest rate, and t represents the time in years.

Ask students to write a polynomial representing the total amount of money each of them will save after six years. Then have them write another polynomial to represent the total amount of money their group will save in two years. Ask students to find the amount of money each will have individually, and in their groups, if the bank is paying 5.5% annually. Which will be the greater amount? Have them explain in detail their reasoning.

Ask each group to create its own problem involving polynomials representing savings accumulated over several years. Once the groups have completed and solved their own created problems, have groups switch with another group to work each other's problem.

Goofin' With Golf

Why did the golfer need a new club?

To find out, add the polynomials below. Write the problem number in front of the corresponding answer listed in the table. To spell out the words at the bottom of the page, refer to the table and write the code letter that corresponds to the problem number given.

1. $(2x^2 - 7x + 6) + (^-3x^2 + 7x)$

2. $(x^2 + 2x) + (2x^2 - 3x + 4)$

3. $(3x^2 + 2x - 4) + (^-x^2 + 2x - 3)$

4. $(4x^2 - 5x + 4) + (^-4x^2 + 5x - 4)$

5. $(5x^2 + 3x - 5) + (2x^2 - 5x + 7)$

6. $(3x^2 + 2x - 7) + (^-2x^2 + 15)$

7. $(x^2 + 5x + 13) + (^-3x^2 + 2x - 8)$

8. $(3 + 2x + x^2) + (5 - 8x + x^2)$

9. $(5x^2 - 4) + (3x^2 + 8x + 4)$

10. $(^-7 - x + 7x^2) + (11 + x^2)$

11. $(4x^2 - 7x - 2) + (2x^2 - 9x + 4)$

12. $(7 - 5x + 6x^2) + (11 - x - 5x^2)$

Code Letter	Problem #	Answer
A		$8 - 6x + 2x^2$
B		$2x^2 + 4x - 7$
C		$6x^2 - 16x + 2$
D		$^-x^2 + 6$
E		$x^2 + 2x + 8$
H		$18 - 6x + x^2$
I		0
L		$3x^2 - x + 4$
N		$^-2x^2 + 7x + 5$
O		$4 - x + 8x^2$
S		$7x^2 - 2x + 2$
U		$8x^2 + 8x$

___ ___ ___ ___ ___ ___ ___   ___ ___   ___ ___ ___
3   6   11   8   9   5   6   12   6   12   8   1

                                                              !

___ ___ ___ ___ ___   ___ ___   ___ ___ ___
8   12   10   2   6   4   7   10   7   6

FS122010 Algebra Made Simple ▪ © Carson-Dellos

Presidential Power

In 1961, at the age of 43 years and 236 days, this President became the youngest elected President in United States history. What is the name of this famous man?

To find out, solve each problem. From the list of answers provided, circle the letters that are next to the matching solutions. Write the letters in front of their corresponding problem numbers to spell out the answer.

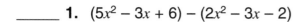

_____ **1.** $(5x^2 - 3x + 6) - (2x^2 - 3x - 2)$

_____ **2.** $(^-3x^2 - 6x + 2) - (^-4x^2 - x - 7)$

_____ **3.** $(6x^2 - 7x + 1) - (5x^2 - 3x - 2)$

_____ **4.** $(5x^2 + 7x + 2) - (^-5x^2 + 7x - 3)$

_____ **5.** $(2x^2 - 6x + 5) - (5x^2 - 6x - 3)$

_____ **6.** $(5x^2 + 4) - (x^2 - 3x + 2)$

_____ **7.** $(3x^2 - 7x + 2) - (x^2 + 8x + 5)$

_____ **8.** $(3x^2 - 8) - (5x^2 + 2x + 7)$

_____ **9.** $(6x^2 - 3x - 7) - (5x^2 + 2x + 3)$

_____ **10.** $(7x^2 - x - 7) - (x^2 + 11)$

_____ **11.** $(5x^2 + 3x) - (2x^2 - 8x + 4)$

_____ **12.** $(4x + 1) - (x^2 - 2x + 3)$

N. $^-2x^2 - 2x - 15$ **A.** $3x^2 - 1$ **N.** $10x^2 + 5$ **G.** $x^2 + 10$

O. $x^2 - 5x + 9$ **J.** $3x^2 + 8$ **E.** $2x^2 - 15x - 3$ **K.** $4x^2 + 3x + 2$

D. $3x^2 + 11x - 4$ **Y.** $^-x^2 + 6x - 2$ **H.** $x^2 - 4x + 3$ **N.** $x^2 - 5x - 10$

F. $^-3x^2 + 8$ **B.** $^-x^2 - 7x - 7$ **L.** $x - 5$ **E.** $6x^2 - x - 18$

Answer: _____

Hiking Through Math

Imagine you and your friends were hiking for several days in the mountains. Why were you never tired?

To find out, simplify each expression by multiplying. Match each problem to its solution. Write the letter corresponding to its solution above each problem number at the bottom of the page to spell out the answer.

1. $(x + 1)(2x + 2)$

2. $(x + 3)(x - 2)$

3. $(4x + 7)(3x - 8)$

4. $(x - 3)(x + 4)$

5. $(3x + 11)(5x - 2)$

6. $(2x + 3)(x^2 + 3x + 8)$

7. $(2x + 5)(3x^2 - 8x + 7)$

8. $(3x - 5)(5x + 2)$

9. $(13x - 3)(13x + 3)$

10. $(3x + 9)^2$

11. $(4x - 2)(4x + 2)$

12. $(2x - 1)(x + 8)$

13. $(7x + 2)(5x + 1)$

14. $(2x^2 + 7x - 11)(3x - 5)$

15. $(4x + 5)^2$

L. $15x^2 + 49x - 22$

T. $9x^2 + 54x + 81$

I. $2x^2 + 15x - 8$

O. $x^2 + x - 6$

P. $6x^3 - x^2 - 26x + 35$

H. $6x^3 + 11x^2 - 68x + 55$

E. $2x^3 + 9x^2 + 25x + 24$

N. $16x^2 - 4$

U. $12x^2 - 11x - 56$

T. $16x^2 + 40x + 25$

S. $x^2 + x - 12$

Y. $2x^2 + 4x + 2$

G. $35x^2 + 17x + 2$

T. $15x^2 - 19x - 10$

A. $169x^2 - 9$

$\overline{}\ \overline{}\ \overline{}\quad \overline{}\ \overline{}\ \overline{}\ \overline{}\ \overline{}\quad \overline{}\ \overline{}\quad \overline{}\ \overline{}\ \overline{}\ \overline{}\ \overline{}$**!**

 1   2   3   4   5   6   7   8   9   10   11 12 13 14 15

FS122010 Algebra Made Simple ▪ © Carson-Dellos

Fresh Start

What is the name of the first state to accept the Constitution, therefore making it the first state in the United States?

To find out, factor each polynomial. Shade in the boxes that contain your solutions. Read across the unshaded boxes to identify the answer to the stately question.

1. $16x^2 - 25$

2. $x^2 - 16$

3. $4x^2 - 1$

4. $4x^2 + 36x + 81$

5. $9x^2 - 24x + 16$

6. $49x^2 + 42x + 9$

7. $x^2 + 7x + 12$

8. $x^2 - 5x - 24$

9. $x^2 + 3x - 180$

10. $7x^2 + 22x + 3$

11. $4x^2 - 4x - 35$

12. $6x^2 + 19x + 10$

B	D	K	E
$(2x + 9)^2$	$(x + 4)(x + 2)$	$(x - 8)(x + 3)$	$(9 - x)(10 - x)$
V	**L**	**P**	**A**
$(2x - 7)(2x + 5)$	$(3x - 5)(3x + 6)$	$(4x + 5)(4x - 5)$	$(5x - 1)(5x + 1)$
F	**T**	**W**	**I**
$(7x + 3)^2$	$(x - 12)(x + 15)$	$(x - 3)(x + 7)$	$(x + 4)(x - 4)$
A	**U**	**C**	**R**
$(9x + 2)^2$	$(3x - 4)^2$	$(x + 3)(x + 4)$	$(x - 2)^2$
S	**E**	**H**	**G**
$(2x + 1)(2x - 1)$	$(2x + 1)^2$	$(3x + 2)(2x + 5)$	$(7x + 1)(x + 3)$

Answer: _____

What's Up Doc?

Why did the math book have to go see a doctor?

To find out, find the solution(s) to each quadratic equation. To spell out the answer to the riddle, write the letter of each problem above its answer(s).

A. $x^2 - 24x + 144 = 0$

B. $x^2 - 2x - 15 = 0$

D. $2x^2 + 18x + 28 = 0$

E. $x^2 - 5x - 36 = 0$

H. $x^2 - 2x - 8 = 0$

I. $x^2 - 5x - 14 = 0$

L. $7x^2 - 70x + 175 = 0$

M. $3x^2 - 3x - 60 = 0$

O. $x^2 - x - 56 = 0$

P. $x^2 - 64 = 0$

R. $x^2 - 2x - 35 = 0$

S. $x^2 - 9 = 0$

T. $x^2 - x - 6 = 0$

$\overline{}$ $\overline{}$ $\overline{}$ $\overline{}$ $\overline{}$
$x = {}^-2, 7$ $x = {}^-2, 3$ $x = {}^-2, 4$ $x = 12$ $x = {}^-2, {}^-7$

$\overline{}$ $\overline{}$ $\overline{}$ $\overline{}$ $\overline{}$ $\overline{}$ $\overline{}$ $\overline{}$ **!**
$x = 8, {}^-8$ $x = {}^-5, 7$ $x = {}^-7, 8$ $x = {}^-3, 5$ $x = 5$ $x = 9, {}^-4$ $x = {}^-4, 5$ $x = {}^-3, 3$

Page 3

1. 21   2. 5   3. 27
4. 13   5. 7   6. 100
7. 78   8. 54   9. 144
10. 18

thirty-eight

Page 4

A. $^-1$ B. $^-18.4$ C. $^-16$
D. 0   E. $^-6$ H. 4.5
I. $^-2$ K. 2.9   L. $^-30$
M. $^-33$ N. 0   O. 10
P. 2   R. $^-40$ S. $^-21$
T. $^-6.5$

arithmetricks

Page 5

1. 3   2. $^-9$ 3. 12
4. $^-4$ 5. $^-8$ 6. $^-70$
7. $^-16$ 8. $^-150$ 9. $^-19$
10. $^-40$ 11. $^-12$ 12. $^-7$
13. $^-6.7$ 14. $^-26$ 15. $^-22$
16. 0   17. 13   18. 1
19. 20

Written Constitution

Page 6

1. 56   2. $^-100$ 3. $^-33$
4. $^-720$ 5. $42a$ 6. ^-70a
7. $^-156$ 8. ^-400a 9. 0
10. 128   11. $32a$ 12. 96
13. $^-75$ 14. ^-72a 15. $^-450$

Michael, Jackie, Marlon, Jermaine,
Tito

Page 7

1. False, <u>opposite</u> angles of equal
   measure; $5x - 35$
2. False, two sides and two angles
   congruent; $^-5x + 15$
3. True
4. True
5. False, no angles congruent;
   $^-80 + 24x$

Page 8

1. 8   2. 27   3. $^-5$
4. $^-24$ 5. $^-4$ 6. $^-5$
7. $^-6$ 8. $^-3$ 9. 4
10. $^-30$ 11. $^-48$ 12. 108
13. $^-6$ 14. $^-144$ 15. 50

20 years old

Page 11

1. $12x$ 2. $8x$ 3. $13x$
4. $25x$ 5. $66x$ 6. $5x$
7. x 8. $9x$ 9. ^-20y
10. $41x - 40y$ 11. $23x - 34y$
12. $3x + 3y$ 13. $^-20x - 25y$
14. $^-35x + 5y$ 15. $^-2x - y$
16. $26x - 7y$

They all chipped in!

Page 12

1. 2   2. 3   3. $^-3$
4. 8   5. $^-11$ 6. 4
7. $^-28$ 8. 16   9. $^-2$
10. $^-1$ 11. $^-41$

twenty-eight

Page 13

1. G: $^-32$; E: $^-12$
2. A: 10; L: 14
3. V: 4; R: $^-12$
4. I: $^-7$; O: $^-18$
5. S: 10; T: $^-5$
6. F: 2; P: 6
7. Y: 3; R: 4
8. A: 3; E: 5
9. S: 10; M: 9
10. B: $^-2$; L: 9
11. I: $^-2$; E: 0
12. Y: $^-6$; R: $^-12$

Elvis Presley

Page 14

1. $^-4$ 2. $^-3$ 3. 3   4. $^-11$
5. $^-8$ 6. 4   7. $^-2$ 8. 2
9. 28   10. $^-12$

Rhode Island

Page 15

1. $y = ^-x + 4$ 2. $y = x - 3$
3. $y = x + 1$ 4. $y = ^-4x + 10$
5. $y = ^-6x - 12$ 6. $y = 8x + 7$
7. $y = 2x + 9$ 8. $y = 3x + 11$
9. $y = 13x - 4$ 10. $y = ^-2x + 3$
11. $y = 3x - 4$ 12. $y = 3x + 4$
13. $y = ^-x + 1$

five after nine

Page 18

million-air

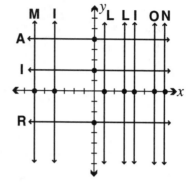

Page 19

1. $(^-3, ^-3)$ 2. $(1, ^-8)$ 3. $(^-1, ^-3)$
4. $(^-1, 1)$ 5. $(1, 5)$ 6. $(^-5, 2)$
7. $(1, ^-1)$ 8. $(^-5, ^-7)$ 9. $(8, 4)$

McDonald's Corporation

Page 20

1. S   2. O   3. A   4. P
5. B   6. U   7. B   8. B
9. L   10. E

soap bubble

Page 21

H. $x = 5, y = 3$
O. $x = 7, y = ^-3$
E. $x = ^-4, y = 16$
I. $x = ^-3, y = ^-10$
Y. $x = ^-2, y = 2$
N. $x = 5, y = ^-3$
E. $x = 8, y = ^-4$
G. $x = ^-8, y = ^-12$
T. $x = ^-3, y = 7$

eighty-one

Page 22

1. 2   2. 1   3. $^-4$ 4. 5
5. $^-1$ 6. 0   7. 3   8. $^-6$
9. undefined   10. $^-7$ 11. 4
12. $^-2$ 13. 7

To earn your degrees!

Page 23

1. $^-3$, falling
2. $^-1$, falling
3. 3, rising
4. undefined, vertical
5. $^-2$, falling
6. 6, rising
7. 0, horizontal
8. $^-6$, falling

9. ⁻5, falling
10. undefined, vertical
11. 4, rising
12. ⁻4, falling
3 hours, 6 minutes

Page 24

1. E
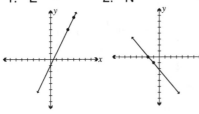

2. N

3. S
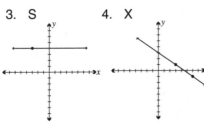

4. X

5. Y
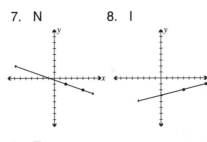

6. I

7. N
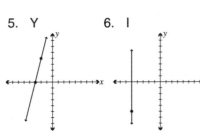

8. I

9. T
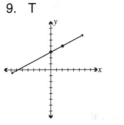

ninety-six

Page 25

1. $y = ⁻x + 4$, $m = ⁻1$, $b = 4$
2. $y = ⁻3x - 7$, $m = ⁻3$, $b = ⁻7$
3. $y = ⁻5x + 9$, $m = ⁻5$, $b = 9$
4. $y = x - 4$, $m = 1$, $b = ⁻4$
5. $y = 3x + 3$, $m = 3$, $b = 3$
6. $y = ⁻½x - 3$, $m = ⁻½$, $b = ⁻3$
7. $y = x - 11$, $m = 1$, $b = ⁻11$

8. $y = 2x - 4$, $m = 2$, $b = ⁻4$
9. $y = 2x - 6$, $m = 2$, $b = ⁻6$
10. $y = ⅓x + 5$, $m = ⅓$, $b = 5$
square feet

Page 26

Greenland

Page 29

1. $y = 2x + 5$ 2. $y = ⁻½x + 7$
3. $y = ⁻4x - 7$ 4. $y = 2$
5. $y = ½x - 3$ 6. $y = 2x$
7. $y = ⁻5x + 2$ 8. $y = 7x + 4$
9. $y = x - 2$ 10. $y = ⁻x - 1$
Los Angeles

Page 30

F. $y = ⁻3x + 6$, $b = 6$
U. $y = 2x - 5$, $b = ⁻5$
R. $y = 3x - 7$, $b = ⁻7$
F. $y = ⁻2x + 4$, $b = 4$
R. $y = ⁻¾x + 3$, $b = 3$
F. $y = 2x - 8$, $b = ⁻8$
U. $y = ⅘x + 5$, $b = 5$
F. $y = ⁻3x + 0$, $b = 0$
"Ruff, Ruff!"

Page 31

N. $y = ⁻³⁄₂x + 3$ S. $y = ⁻x + 3$
W. $y = ⁻5x$ Y. $y = 4x - 15$
X. $y = 3x - 13$ T. $y = ⁻1$
E. $y = 3x - 10$ I. $y = ½x - 1$
T. $y = 2x$
twenty-six

Page 32

cookie

Page 33

N. $4x + y = 4$
C. $x + y = ⁻7$
S. $⁻6x + y = 3$
T. $⁻6x + y = ⁻7$
D. $5x + y = 8$
A. $⁻8x + y = 11$
E. $⁻4x - 3y = 2$
N. $8x + 7y = 3$
E. $3x - y = ⁻8$
P. $9x - 5y = 6$
L. $⁻4x - 4y = ⁻5$
E. $⁻6x - 5y = 7$
U. $⁻10x + 11y = 2$
D. $3x - 7y = 18$
dependent claus

Page 34

1. $⁻2x + y = 1$ 2. $⁻2x + y = ⁻3$
3. $⁻x + y = ⁻9$ 4. $4x + y = 8$
5. $⁻⁵⁄₂x + y = 4$ 6. $8x + 2y = 4$
7. $5x - y = 3$ 8. $x + 3y = 3$
nineteen

Page 35

1. T   2. H   3. E   4. M
5. I   6. S   7. S   8. I
9. S   10. S   11. I   12. P
13. P   14. I
the Mississippi

Page 38

1. $y = 0, ⁻3, ⁻6$
2. $y = ⁻1, 4$
3. $y = ⁻2, ⁻6, ⁻9$
4. $y = ⁻9, ⁻6, ⁻2, 4, ⁻8, ⁻2, 4, ⁻4$
5. $y = 12, 8, 0$
Put on its stinking cap!

Page 39

1. $x = 2, ⁻6$ 2. $x = ⁻14, 8$
3. $x = 23, ⁻5$ 4. $x = 5, ⁻1$
5. $x = 13, ⁻15$ 6. $x = ⁻3, 21$
7. $x = ⁻14, 16$ 8. $x = ⁻7, ⁻5$
9. $x = 15, ⁻21$ 10. $x = ⁻2, 6$
11. $x = 8, ⁻2$ 12. $x = 0, 12$
Robert Wadlow

Page 40

1. (3, 6)   2. (⁻4, ⁻5)
3. (1, 0)   4. (⁻9, ⁻9)
5. (2, 3)   6. (0, 4)
7. (⁻1, ⁻1)   8. (0, 0)
9. (⁻8, 0)   10. (0, 9)
He knew a short cut!

Page 41

1. $V = (⁻3, ⁻2)$ 2. $V = (6, 5)$
3. $V = (⁻2, 1)$ 4. $V = (5, 4)$
5. $V = (⁻1, ⁻1)$ 6. $V = (4, 4)$
France

Page 42

1. $V = (2, 0)$, opens down
2. $V = (1, 3)$, opens up
3. $V = (⁻4, ⁻1)$, opens down
4. $V = (0, 5)$, opens down
5. $V = (2, 4)$, opens up
6. $V = (⁻3, 0)$, opens down
7. $V = (0, 0)$, opens up

FS122010 Algebra Made Simple ▪ © Carson-Dellosa

8. V = (4, ⁻2), opens down
9. V = (5, 1), opens up
0. V = (3, ⁻5), opens down

our

Page 43

T. $x < 10$ A. $x \geq 19$
I. $x > ⁻22$ O. $x > ⁻2$
A. $x \geq 11$ E. $x < ⁻14$
L. $x \leq 25$ E. $x < ⁻8$
H. $x \geq 2$ N. $x > 47$
H. $x > ⁻3$ E. $x \geq 6$
C. $x > ⁻6$ N. $x \leq ⁻2$

An ace in the hole!

Page 44

1. $x \leq ⁻2$ or $x > 8$
2. $1 \leq x \leq 7$
3. $⁻10 < x < 10$
4. $x < ⁻7$ or $x \geq 8$
5. $⁻3 \leq x < 5$
6. $x < 2$ or $x > 5$
7. $x \geq 9$ or $x \leq 7$
8. $x < ⁻3$ or $x \geq 5$

Michigan

Page 45

A. $x < 1$ or $x > 3$
W. $⁻4 \leq x \leq ⁻1$
T. $⁻6 < x < 3$
Y. $x \leq ⁻3$ or $x \geq 7$
A. $⁻3 \leq x \leq 6$
D. $⁻11 < x < 3$
A. $\frac{1}{2} \leq x \leq 2$

data-way

Page 46

1. yes 2. no 3. yes
4. no 5. yes 6. yes
7. no 8. yes 9. no
0. yes

six

Page 47

1.   2.

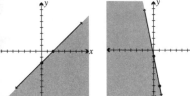

3. 4.

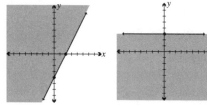

5. 6.

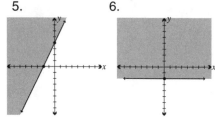

7. 8.

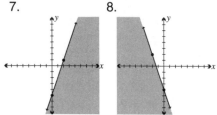

9. 10.

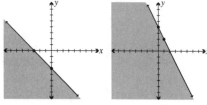

three days

Page 50

1. (4, 5) 2. (1, 8) 3. (17, 10)
4. (3, 3) 5. (3, ⁻1) 6. (⁻6, 8)
7. (3, 5) 8. (3, 4) 9. (5, 2)
10. (12, 1) For a tune-up!

Page 51

S. (2, 1) M. (1, 1) L. (3, 10)
X. (⁻3, 2) I. (6, 0) I. (⁻6, 8)
S. (2, 5) E. (⁻3, ⁻5)

six miles

Page 52

1. (⁻2, ⁻2) 2. (⁻3, 0) 3. (4, 0)
4. (0, 1) 5. (2, ⁻2) 6. (2, 3)
7. (⁻1, ⁻1) 8. (4, ⁻5) 9. (3, 7)

John Wayne

Page 53

1. (1, ⁻½) 2. (⁻5, 2) 3. (2, 2)
4. (1, 0) 5. (1, 1) 6. (⁻7, 3)
7. (⁻3, 0) 8. (2, 3) 9. (4, 0)

seven gold

Page 54

1. Has many solutions
2. Has no solution
3. Has no solution
4. Has many solutions
5. Has no solution
6. Has many solutions
7. Has no solution
8. Has no solution
9. Has many solutions

Bugs Bunny

Page 55

1. Quadrants I, II, III, IV
2. Quadrant II
3. Quadrants I, II, III
4. Quadrants I, III, IV
5. Quadrants I, II
6. Quadrant I
7. Quadrants I, IV
8. Quadrants II, III

Thriller (Michael Jackson)

Page 58

1. $3x^5$ 2. $32x^5$ 3. x^{15}
4. $30x^6$ 5. $⁻42x^7$ 6. $⁻x^4y^7$
7. $72x^3y^2$ 8. $⁻64x^{12}$ 9. $⁻3x^9y^7$
10. $x^{14}y^2$ 11. $8x^{12}y^3$

Garfield the Cat

Page 59

1. x 2. $⁻x/9$
3. 1 4. $1/(2x)$
5. $81y^2$ 6. $⁻3/(xy)$
7. $(⁻4x)/(3y^3)$ 8. $⁻2y^3$
9. $9x^6$ thirty-six

Page 60

1. $2/x^5$ 2. $⁻3/y$
3. $(2y^3)/x^5$ 4. $1/4$
5. $8x^5$ 6. $(⁻4y^9)/x^4$
7. $(⁻3y^6)/x^4$ 8. 1

Seinfeld

Page 61

1. 0.00031
2. 804,000
3. 0.0046
4. 2,000
5. 56,200,000
6. 0.00000703
7. 5.62×10^6
8. 7.8×10^{-6}

9. 4.01×10^2
10. 9.145×10^7
11. 6.0×10^{-7}
12. 1.23×10^5
Elvis Presley

Page 64
1. 5   2. $^-8$ 3. 0.4
4. $^-11$ 5. ½   6. $^-7/4$
7. ±7   8. ±10   9. ±4
10. ±15   11. 0   12. ±⅓
Pan-American Highway

Page 65
1. 15   2. 6.32   3. 10
4. 21   5. 24   6. 9.54
7. 30   8. 3.16   9. 9.80
10. 40
fifty-seven

Page 66
D. $x = ^-3, ^-4$ T. $x = ^-6, 2$
R. $x = ^-8, ^-2$ S. $x = ^-4, 1$
O. $x = 1, 6$ S. $x = ^-3, 8$
A. $x = 2, 6$ L. $x = ^-3, 5$
G. $x = ^-2, ^-4$
gold stars

Page 67
1. $V = (^-3, ^-1)$, up
2. $V = (2, ^-3)$, up
3. $V = (^-4, 1)$, down
4. $V = (0, 0)$, down
5. $V = (^-3, 1)$, down
6. $V = (2, 1)$, up
7. $V = (0, ^-4)$, down
8. $V = (^-3, ^-9)$, up
9. $V = (2, 3)$, up
10. $V = (^-3, 2)$, down
five years old

Page 70
1. $^-x^2 + 6$
2. $3x^2 - x + 4$
3. $2x^2 + 4x - 7$
4. 0
5. $7x^2 - 2x + 2$
6. $x^2 + 2x + 8$
7. $^-2x^2 + 7x + 5$
8. $8 - 6x + 2x^2$
9. $8x^2 + 8x$
10. $4 - x + 8x^2$

11. $6x^2 - 16x + 2$
12. $18 - 6x + x^2$
Because he had a hole in one!

Page 71
1. $3x^2 + 8$
2. $x^2 - 5x + 9$
3. $x^2 - 4x + 3$
4. $10x^2 + 5$
5. $^-3x^2 + 8$
6. $4x^2 + 3x + 2$
7. $2x^2 - 15x - 3$
8. $^-2x^2 - 2x - 15$
9. $x^2 - 5x - 10$
10. $6x^2 - x - 18$
11. $3x^2 + 11x - 4$
12. $^-x^2 + 6x - 2$
John F. Kennedy

Page 72
1. $2x^2 + 4x + 2$
2. $x^2 + x - 6$
3. $12x^2 - 11x - 56$
4. $x^2 + x - 12$
5. $15x^2 + 49x - 22$
6. $2x^3 + 9x^2 + 25x + 24$
7. $6x^3 - x^2 - 26x + 35$
8. $15x^2 - 19x - 10$
9. $169x^2 - 9$
10. $9x^2 + 54x + 81$
11. $16x^2 - 4$
12. $2x^2 + 15x - 8$
13. $35x^2 + 17x + 2$
14. $6x^3 + 11x^2 - 68x + 55$
15. $16x^2 + 40x + 25$
You slept at night!

Page 73
1. $(4x + 5)(4x - 5)$
2. $(x + 4)(x - 4)$
3. $(2x + 1)(2x - 1)$
4. $(2x + 9)^2$
5. $(3x - 4)^2$
6. $(7x + 3)^2$
7. $(x + 3)(x + 4)$
8. $(x - 8)(x + 3)$
9. $(x - 12)(x + 15)$
10. $(7x + 1)(x + 3)$
11. $(2x - 7)(2x + 5)$
12. $(3x + 2)(2x + 5)$
Delaware

Page 74
A. $x = 12$ B. $x = ^-3, 5$
D. $x = ^-2, ^-7$ E. $x = 9, ^-4$
H. $x = ^-2, 4$ I. $x = ^-2, 7$
L. $x = 5$ M. $x = ^-4, 5$
O. $x = ^-7, 8$ P. $x = 8, ^-8$
R. $x = ^-5, 7$ S. $x = ^-3, 3$
T. $x = ^-2, 3$
It had problems!